KV-576-905

Ripley's SPORTS

Believe It or Not!®

Ripley PUBLISHING

a Jim Pattison Company

TWISTS

Written by Geoff Tibballs
Consultant Stewart Newport

PUBLISHING

Publisher Anne Marshall

Editorial Director Rebecca Miles
Project Editor Lisa Regan
Editor Rosie Alexander
Assistant Editor Charlotte Howell
Picture Researchers James Proud, Charlotte Howell
Proofreader Judy Barratt
Indexer Hilary Bird

Art Director Sam South
Senior Designer Michelle Cannatella
Design Rocket Design (East Anglia) Ltd
Reprographics Juice Creative Ltd

www.ripleybooks.com

Copyright ©2010 by Ripley Entertainment Inc.

First published in Great Britain in 2010 by Random House Books, Random House, 20 Vauxhall Bridge Road, London SW1V 2SA www.randomhouse.co.uk

This edition 2013

Ripley's Sports and *Ripley's Human Body* also available as individual volumes.

Addresses for companies within The Random House Group Limited can be found at: www.randomhouse.co.uk/offices.htm

The Random House Group Limited Reg. No. 954009

All rights reserved. Ripley's, Believe It or Not! and Ripley's Believe It or Not! are registered trademarks of Ripley Entertainment Inc.

ISBN 9780099567981

10 9 8 7 6 5 4 3 2 1

No part of this publication may be reproduced in whole or in part, or stored in a retrieval system, or transmitted in any form or by any means, electronic, mechanical, photocopying, recording, or otherwise, without written permission from the publisher. For information regarding permission, write to VP Intellectual Property, Ripley Entertainment Inc., Suite 188, 7576 Kingspointe Parkway, Orlando, Florida 32819. e-mail: publishing@ripleys.com

A CIP catalogue record for this book is available from the British Library

Manufactured in China
in April 2013 by Leo Paper
1st printing

WARNING
Some of the activities in this book are undertaken by experts and should not be attempted without adequate training and supervision.

PUBLISHER'S NOTE
While every effort has been made to verify the accuracy of the entries in this book, the Publishers cannot be held responsible for any errors contained herein. They would be glad to receive any information from readers.

CONTENTS

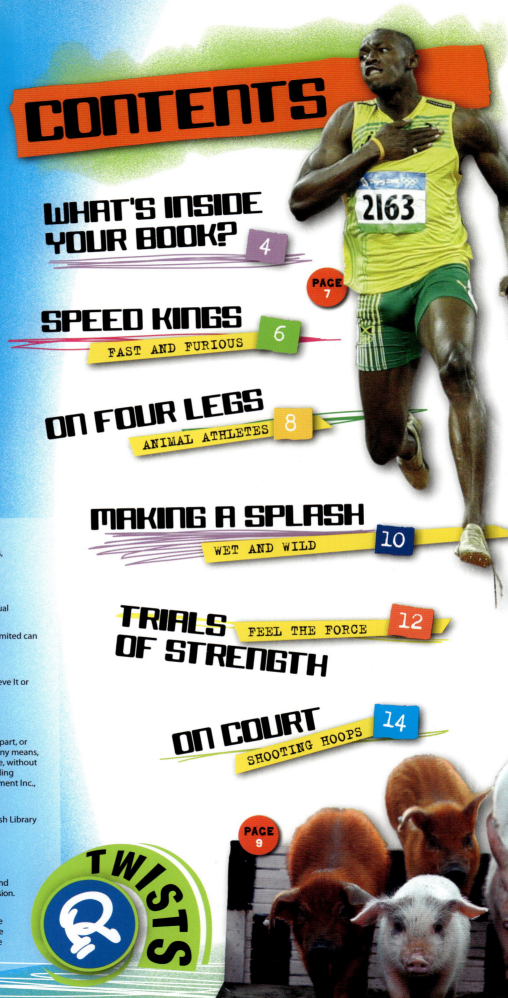

PAGE 9

TWISTS

PAGE
13

3

WORLD OF SPORT

So you think you know about sport? Well, prepare to learn even more! Top sports attract millions of spectators and billions of pounds, and bring together countries across the globe to play, watch and shout about their favourite games and competitions.

Sport isn't just about big money, clubs and players. Some sports are played and watched by only a few people, but are just as much fun. So, if you're not into ball games, this book will introduce you to tug-of-war, BMX racing, and even worm charming. There's something here for everyone…

WHAT'S INSIDE YOUR BOOK?

Do the twist

Take a look…each page is packed with sporting superstars, amazing achievements, and of course, crazy pastimes that don't get a mention in other sports books. That's what a Twists book is all about!

TWISTS

twist it!

Don't forget to look out for the 'twist it!' column on some pages. Twist the book to read snappy sports stories from all around the world; if you're feeling super sporty then read it standing on your head!

HEAD KICKS

Welsh footie fan Steve Thatcher named his son after all the players in his favourite team, Cardiff City, it means young Sam has 12 middle names!

An annual football match called the Calcio takes place in Florence, Italy, between two teams of 27 players dressed in 16th-century costume. It is a rough game, and players are allowed to elbow, kick, and even head butt each other!

Important football matches often attract crowds of over 70,000 people, but the 1950 World Cup final between Brazil and Uruguay was watched by nearly 200,000 spectators.

Some football matches are decided by penalty shoot-outs, where eight kicks are often enough to get a result. At the end of a 2005 Namibian Cup tie in Africa, the penalty contest went on for an incredible 48 kicks and lasted nearly an hour!

SPEEDY SPORTS

Sport isn't all about speed – but speed certainly makes sport exciting! See what's fastest in the world of sport…

Motorbike 580 km/h

Formula 1 Car 414 km/h

Learn fab fast facts to go with the cool pictures.

Ripley explains some of the science and know-how behind your favourite sports.

Say what? Oh, so that's what that word means...

Twists are all about 'Believe It or Not!' – amazing facts, feats, and things that will make you go 'Wow!'

Look for the Ripley 'R' to find out even more than you knew before!

SURF'S UP

RIDING THE WAVES

It's not only waves that are a danger to surfers. Each year as many as 80 surfers are attacked by sharks.

84 surfers rode the same wave at the same time off the coast of Brazil in 2007!

Have you ever wished you could ride a wave on a surfboard? Some waves are huge – over 20 m high. That's more than four times the height of an adult giraffe! That just makes it even more of a challe... You can surf a wave ...ing down – and some ...on the same wave for half an ...you just do what you enjoy.

...18th century – used planks of ...weight polyurethane for ...e California, Florid... ...abed and strong...

Ripley explains...

You catch a wave by pushing the water towards the back of the surfboard with your hands, moving you forwards. As you ride on the wave the water rises beneath you and pushes you forwards faster and faster. All the time gravity is trying to push you down, while buoyancy is pushing you up.

PLAIN SAILING

Windsurfers attach a sail to their surfboards. When the wind blows into the sail from behind, it makes the board go faster- sometimes up to 100 km/h! Windsurfers can perform amazing stunts, jumps and spins.

RIDING HIGH

Kite surfers use wind power to help them speed across the water and soar up to 50 m in the air. They stand on a board and hold on to a large controllable kite. The aim is to do tricks such as jumps, spins and even somersaults, and to see how high and long they can jump off waves.

SAY WHAT?

CATCH A WAVE

This is when you launch yourself into the path of a suitable wave.

Kite surfers can go great distances when the wind is behind them. In 2006, UK kite surfer Kirsty Jones travelled 225 km from Lanzarote in the Canary Islands to Morocco.

Donald 'DJ' Dettloff has created a colourful fence from more than 700 surfboards near his home in Hawaii.

Ripley's Believe It or Not!

Lauren Miller's dog Auggie liked to do tricks with tennis balls. He could pick up five in his mouth at the same time!

Motorbike Wheelie	Ostrich	Camel	Racehorse	Human (sprinter)
225 km/h	72 km/h	64 km/h	64 km/h	37 km/h

SPEED KINGS

The cars reach speeds of nearly 400 km/h on the straights.

Imagine flying a plane at over 3,000 km/h. Or riding a motorbike at 600 km/h. Or driving a speedboat at 500 km/h. Wow! Ever since vehicles were invented, people have wanted them to go as fast as possible. We love speed. That's why we dream of one day racing in NASCAR or driving in a Formula-1 race. The cars there can go from 0 to 160 km/h and back to 0 in under five seconds.

Jamaica's Usain Bolt doesn't need an engine to go fast. He can run at amazing speeds. In 100-metre races he averages just under 40 km/h but for a few strides he actually reaches 50 km/h. That's the speed limit for a car in most towns!

Three drivers (AJ Foyt, Al Unser and Rick Mears) have won four Indy 500s.

The Indy 500 is probably the most famous motor race in the world. About 400,000 people turn up to watch, and millions more see it on TV in more than 160 countries. The 500-mile (805-kilometre) race takes place every year at the oval-shaped Indianapolis Motor Speedway in Indiana.

CRAZY CORNERING

As they go round corners, motorbike racers lean their machines at almost impossible angles of 50 degrees without falling off. The riders have their knee just a few centimetres off the ground to work out how much they can lean before their bike loses balance and topples over.

Fire-proof balaclava

HIGH SPEED FURNACE

Formula-1 drivers need to be amazingly fit. The temperature in the car reaches 50°C and drivers get very hot beneath their fire-proof overalls. They lose an average of 2 kg in body weight during each race. When braking and cornering, the pull on the driver's neck is so great that it feels as if their head wants to roll off their shoulders!

Flame-resistant driving suit

When the Indy 500 was first raced in 1911, the track was made up of 3.2 million bricks, earning it the nickname 'The Brickyard'.

twist it!

In 2005, Australian Matt Mingay did a motorbike wheelie at a speed of 225 km/h.

The 1972 Bandama Car Rally in West Africa was so tough that none of the 52 starters finished the race.

CG Mouch of Los Angeles fitted the front end of a 750cc Honda motorcycle to the rear end of his lawn mower to create a 'chopper mower' that could mow the lawn at up to 15 km/h.

English farmer George Shields drives a garden shed that can do 90 km/h. He once drove it all the way from one end of Britain to the other. That's nearly 1,300 km.

The first car race was run in France from Paris to Rouen in 1894. The average winning speed was just over 17 km/h!

MOTORHEADS

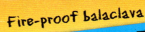

FASCINATING FACT! FASCINATING FACT! FASCINATING FACT!

LIGHTNING BOLT

Jamaican runner Usain Bolt won the 100 metres at the 2008 Beijing Olympics in an incredible 9.69 seconds — despite slowing down to celebrate and having his left shoelace undone!

2163

F1

ON FOUR LEGS

ANIMAL ATHLETES

Racehorses are bred for speed. These thoroughbreds, as they are known, can gallop at up to 65 km/h. Horse-racing dates back nearly 3,000 years to the ancient Greeks who added the spectacular sport of chariot racing to the Olympics in 680BC. Horse-racing is so popular today that in Switzerland there is even a horse race on ice, run on a frozen lake.

There are also races for animals that you might not think are built for speed, such as camels, armadillos, pigs and sheep. Whatever the animal, there is probably a race for it somewhere in the world. We don't only race animals. We wrestle them, we ski behind them, and in parts of Asia polo is played on elephants instead of horses.

HORSE POWER

In the Palio, which takes place twice each summer, horses race at breakneck speed three times around the main square in Siena, Italy – and the riders don't even have saddles to sit on. No wonder so many fall off!

Around 60,000 people squeeze into the square to watch the colourful race.

The Palio was first raced in 1656 and has remained largely the same ever since.

A bank of mattresses is positioned to protect the horses and riders from the walls of a café at a turn known as the 'corner of death'.

Jockeys are usually small, but they also have to be strong, because racehorses can weigh up to 700 kg.

SAY WHAT?

DERBY

A derby is a type of race. The original derby was a horse race run in Epsom, England, and was named after the Earl of Derby who founded the event in 1780.

JUMBO POLO

Polo is usually played on horseback but in countries such as Nepal, India and Thailand they play it with elephants. Two people ride each elephant – one to steer the elephant, the other to hit the ball. The mallet used to strike the ball is made of bamboo and can be up to 3.7 m long, depending on the height of the elephant. If a player falls off, it's a long way down!

RACING AROUND

The Frog Derby takes place in Rayne, Louisiana, where kids dress frogs in miniature jockey uniforms! By tapping the ground behind the frogs, they encourage them to hop along the course in leaps and bounds.

At an annual round-up in Stephensville, Wisconsin, participants try to wrestle slippery, squirming pigs to the ground in thick mud.

You may have heard of greyhound racing. Well, in Oklahoma City, they have a dog race with a difference – it's for little dachshunds and it's called the Dachshund Dash.

Back in 1937, a man in England tried to stage cheetah racing as an alternative to greyhounds. The cheetahs showed no interest in running, however, and often just stood still.

twist it!

<< PIG OLYMPICS >>

It's not only humans that have their own Olympics. There is also an Olympic Games for pigs! Miniature pigs run over hurdles, compete in swimming races and play a version of football called pigball, where they chase a ball covered in fish oil with their snouts.

A racehorse named Camarero won 56 races in a row in Puerto Rico between 1953 and 1955.

DESERT DERBY

In the Middle East and Australia, camel racing is a serious sport with big prize money. Top racing camels sell for up to £30,000. Camels can run as fast as 65 km/h in short sprints and can maintain a speed of 30 km/h for an hour. Jockeys need nerves of steel because the camels can sometimes suddenly stop mid-way through a race without warning!

MAKING A SPLASH

WET AND WILD

Water isn't a person's natural element: our lungs need air, we don't have webbed feet or hands, and we aren't designed for speed in the way that a shark or a seal is. That hasn't stopped us from taking the plunge, though.

Free divers plummet to depths of more than 180 m using only their finely tuned athlete's bodies. Marathon swimmers race over distances of up to 25 km in lakes, rivers or the ocean. Competition divers perform graceful gymnastics before hitting the water at around 55 km/h. They're all spectacular.

Taking a dive

Competitive divers perform twists or somersaults in mid-air after jumping from a platform up to 10 m above the pool. They have just a split second to get everything right. They must enter the water with their body in a vertical position and their arms extended forward – and without making much of a splash.

PROFESSOR SPLASH

From heights of up to 25 m, Darren Taylor, of Denver, Colorado, dives into tiny, shallow pools, some containing just 30 cm of water! He says the secret is to make a real splash when he lands – that way his fall is cushioned. The impact still leaves his body so bruised that it hurts him to laugh for weeks afterwards.

SAY WHAT?

FREESTYLE

In a freestyle race swimmers can use any style – front crawl, butterfly, backstroke or breaststroke. Most use the front crawl, because it's the fastest.

DIVE IN!

Once a diver has left the board, his or her body must be held in one of four positions.

STRAIGHT: no bend in either the hips or knees.

PIKE: knees straight and the body bent at the waist.

TUCK: the body is curled up in a tight ball.

FREE: a combination of straight, pike or tuck with the legs together.

Absolutely nuts

Twiggy the grey squirrel is nuts about water-skiing. Her Florida trainer, Lou Ann Best, taught her to be towed around an inflatable paddling pool by a remote-controlled model boat at speeds of up to 10 km/h. Twiggy has demonstrated her skills at boat shows across America.

HIGH DIVE

Tom Daley became the world 10-metre platform diving champion in 2009 at the age of just 15. That made him the youngest diver ever to win a title in men's platform diving. He started diving at age seven and was Britain's youngest competitor at the 2008 Olympic Games.

It's never too late to start a sport. As a child, Australia's Ian Thorpe was allergic to chlorine (the chemical used in swimming pools), so he didn't swim in his first race until he was seven. Even then the allergy forced him to swim awkwardly with his head out of water.

SLOW STARTER

His nickname was 'the Thorpedo' because of his speed in the water.

By age 14 Ian Thorpe was representing his country.

11

TRIALS OF STRENGTH

Some people are so strong they can bend iron bars with their head or pull trains with their teeth. Others can lift cars off the ground, tear thick books with their bare hands or pull trucks with their hair. For centuries, people have demonstrated their strength by taking part in competitive combat sports such as boxing, sumo wrestling, judo, taekwondo and karate.

If you don't want to be a real-life muscle man, you could take part in some wackier trials of strength. How about having a go at fish tossing, welly hurling or mobile-phone throwing?

It took Rev. Fast 1 minute 16 seconds to pull the plane 8.8 m with a rope.

The Globemaster weighed a huge 187 tonnes.

The previous record for pulling a plane was 186 tonnes and had stood for 12 years.

He trains for his strong-man challenges by pulling his pickup truck up hills.

Strong stomach

Fitness instructor Ken Richmond has such a sturdy stomach he lets people fire cannon balls at it! He can also survive a cannon ball being dropped on his head and withstand the force of a massive 18,000-kg wrecking ball slamming through a concrete wall and into his amazing abdomen.

PLANE CRAZY

In 2009, Reverend Kevin Fast, of Cobourg, Ontario, Canada, managed to pull an enormous military CC-17 Globemaster airplane across the tarmac at Canadian Forces Base Trenton.

12

FAST MOVER

Ripley's Believe It or Not!

- American martial arts movie star Bruce Lee moved his arms and feet with lightning speed. He was so fast he could snatch a coin off a person's open palm before they could close it, and leave a different coin behind.
- To toughen the skin on his fists, he used to regularly thrust his hands into buckets of rocks and gravel up to 500 times.
- He could break wooden boards that were 15 cm thick with a single punch.
- He could perform one-handed push-ups using only his thumb and index finger.
- He could thrust his fingers through unopened fizzy drink cans.
- He practised his high kicks by jumping up and tapping people on the ear with his foot.

Ripley explains...

Contact points used in Karate

Wrist · Knifehand · Spearhand · Back of the hand · Ball of the foot · Instep

In the Japanese martial art of karate, you can punch or kick but the most famous technique is the knifehand or karate chop. Some people can smash over 30 slabs of concrete with just a single karate chop.

EARS!

Zafar Gill, from Pakistan, can lift 55 kg with one of his ears.

EYES!

Dong Changsheng, from China, once pulled a 1,700-kg minibus carrying two adult passengers... with his eyelids!

Luxembourg's Georges Christen can do just about anything with his teeth. He has towed a 95-tonne ship with them, and bent 368 nails with them in an hour. One stunt saw him stop three 110-horsepower Cessna Sport airplanes from taking off at full power – one with his teeth and two with his arms.

TOUGH TEETH

twist it!

In New Zealand, there is an annual contest to see who can throw a gumboot (wellington boot) the farthest. At the end of the competition, the winner is presented with a Golden Gumboot!

In Michigan in 1997, Samoan heavyweight boxer Jimmy Thunder knocked out Crawford Grimsley after just 1.7 seconds of their fight.

The first Mobile Phone Throwing World Championships were held in Finland in 2000. One of the sport's top throwers is the UK's Chris Hughff who can hurl a phone 95.7 m. That's a real long distance call!

Ed Byrne from England used his bare hands to karate chop through 55 concrete blocks in less than five seconds...and it didn't even hurt!

STRONG STUFF

ON COURT

More than 46 million Americans play volleyball and there are around 800 million players worldwide. In fact, football is the only sport that more people play across the globe. Like basketball, tennis, squash and badminton, volleyball is played on a court. All of these sports require you to be able to run about, have quick reactions, and be very fit. Tennis players can cover 8 km during a match!

Tennis players can also earn a lot of money. The winners of the singles titles at Wimbledon in London (the world's oldest tennis tournament) receive £1 million. Basketball players can earn even more. Some get paid over £13 million a year!

Michael was so feared that opponents would put two or even three men to cover him every time he touched the ball.

GROWTH SPURT

At high school, Michael Jordan was considered too short to play basketball. Then he grew 10 cm one summer, and began the path to superstardom that saw a 1996 sports magazine name him the greatest athlete of the past 50 years. He finished with an incredible career total of 32,292 points, the third highest in league history.

High court

Top tennis players Roger Federer and Andre Agassi needed a head for heights when they played on this court. It was marked out on the helipad of a Dubai hotel 210 m above ground. If a ball sailed out, nobody went to fetch it!

Ripley's Believe It or Not!®

Lauren Miller's dog Auggie liked to do tricks with tennis balls. He could pick up five in his mouth at the same time!

IN A SPIN

Using his hands, feet, knees, and even his mouth, American Bruce Crevier can spin up to 21 basketballs at the same time. He has also spun a single basketball on his fingers for more than 22 hours – that's nearly a whole day!

PLAYING BALL

America's Andy Roddick can serve a tennis ball at 250 km/h – that's as fast as an express train.

A game of volleyball that took place in Amstelveen, the Netherlands, in 2008 lasted 60 hours. That's 2½ days!

Basketball-crazy Mike Campbell made 1,338 free throws in an hour (faster than one throw every three seconds) and over 90 per cent of his shots were successful.

Twin brothers Ettore and Angelo Rosseti played a continuous tennis rally that lasted nearly 15 hours, with a total of 25,944 shots.

Joseph Odhiambo dribbled a basketball through the streets of Houston, Texas, for 26 hours in 2006.

You have to be really fit to play squash. A squash player can burn up to 1,000 calories during a one-hour game. That's almost twice as many than if you were doing push-ups non-stop for the same amount of time. Phew!

twist it!

SMASHING!

Badminton is played by hitting a shuttlecock made either from goose feathers or plastic. Shuttlecocks can be hit very fast. A smash by very fast. Fu Haifeng was China's recorded at 370 km/h.

SISTER ACT

Venus Williams and her younger sister Serena have dominated women's tennis in the 21st century. Between them they have won over 30 Grand Slam tennis titles. At the 1999 Australian Open Venus's dreadlocked hair was docked a point when a string of beads fell from around her court. scattered around the 'was paved at 'the second-fastest US Open, Venus served at 208 km/h – the second-fastest woman's serve ever recorded.

SNOW AND ICE

CHILLS AND THRILLS

If you've ever sped down a hill on a sledge, you'll know how exciting snow can be. Wherever there is suitable snow and ice, sportspeople can be found competing on it. Speed skiers can hit a breathtaking 240 km/h, ski jumpers leap 180 m while sailing through the air at 105 km/h, and teams on bobsleighs hurtle around a steep course of solid ice at 145 km/h. They all know that the slightest mistake could result in a bad injury.

It's not all about speed. There's the gracefulness of ice skating, the elegance of snowboarding, and the rough and tumble of hockey. So if you thought the best thing about snow was building a snowman, you might have to think again.

SNOW TRICKS

Snowboarding is like surfing on snow. Boarders perform lots of tricks. In a U-shaped trench called a halfpipe, they do acrobatic spins and flips and even a trick where they grab their board in mid-air.

DOWNHILL RACERS

Slalom skiers speed down a steep mountain, weaving their way between a series of poles called gates. Nets are placed alongside the course at the most dangerous places but the skiers still have spectacular falls.

LOONY LUGE

Luge is one of the most dangerous sports. Competitors lie down on a fibreglass sledge and hurtle feet-first down an icy track at speeds up to 145 km/h. They wear little protection, their bodies are just centimetres from the ice, and the luge has no brakes!

ICE BOWLING

The coolest game of bowling takes place in Japan. Players roll a bowling ball made of ice along a frozen 5-m lane towards 17-cm-high ice pins.

Between 2003 and 2006, American Rainer Hertrich skied for 1,000 days in a row. He once hiked up an active volcano in Chile because it had more snow to ski down than neighbouring mountains!

WAYNE'S WORLD

Canadian Wayne Gretzky is the only National Hockey League player to total over 200 points (goals and assists) in a season, and he did it four times. He scored over 100 points in 14 consecutive seasons and was so popular that he used to receive 1,000 fan letters every month.

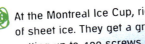

At the Montreal Ice Cup, riders race bicycles over a course of sheet ice. They get a grip on the slippery surface by putting up to 400 screws into the rubber tyres.

THE WALL

UNUSUAL SPORTS

The World Games is held every four years and features several unusual sports that aren't in the Olympics. These include canoe polo, dragon boat racing, climbing, tug of war, roller hockey, and even dancing. If you prefer your sports a little less energetic, have you ever thought about taking up worm charming or cherry pit spitting? There are many weird and wonderful sports that you can try wherever you live.

PULLING POWER

In tug of war, two teams of eight grip tightly on to either end of a 35-m-long rope and use their combined strength to pull their opponents over a line. Tug of war was practised as early as 500BC by Greek athletes and was an Olympic sport until 1920.

MIGHTY MUSCLES

A Japanese bodybuilder flexes her muscles at the 2009 World Games. Nearly 3,000 athletes from 84 countries took part in the Games.

PIE IN THE SKY

A Canadian and two Australians battle to catch the Frisbee during the flying disc competition at the World Games. The sport can be traced back to the Frisbie Pie Company in Connecticut, where workers played a game in which they threw empty pie tins to one another!

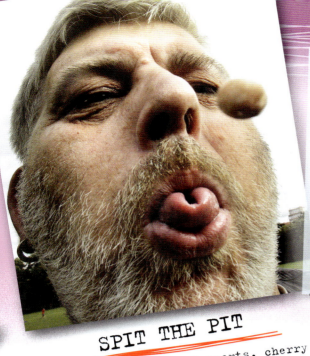

SPORTS CRAZY

At the World Flounder Tramping Championships in Scotland, people catch fish using their bare feet. They wade into the river and when they feel the flat fish wriggling between their toes, they pick it up. The person who catches the most fish is declared the winner.

If you've got something to shout about, you can do it at the National Hollerin' Contest, held each year at Spivey's Corner, North Carolina. Contestants yell as loud as they can for four minutes – you might want to take ear plugs!

At the Sheep Counting Championships of Australia, several hundred sheep are encouraged to run across a field while competitors try to count them.

twist it!

SPIT THE PIT

Like many established sports, cherry pit spitting started as a casual pastime and has developed into a popular event in which people compete at national and international competitions. At the 2006 World Championship in Germany, Franz-Wolfgang Coersten spit a pit an impressive 19.3 m.

THE EARLY BIRD

The World Worm Charming Championships have taken place since 1980 in Willaston, Cheshire, England. Competitors coax earthworms to the surface by wiggling garden forks in the soil or by pouring water on it. The winner is the person who brings the most worms to the surface in half an hour. In 2009, 10-year-old Sophie Smith won the first prize with a grand total of 567.

MOooo

POOOO

POLE POSITION

To be crowned pole-sitting champion, you need a head for heights and a lot of patience. In 2002, Daniel Baraniuk won $20,000 (about £13,000) after spending 196 days and nights (over six months) on top of a 2.5-m-high pole. His closest rival fell off a month earlier!

COW PATTY BINGO

In some rural areas of North America you can play cow patty bingo. A field is divided into numbered squares, and contestants bet on which square the cow will take a poop!

TOUCH DOWN

CATCH AND KICK

Each year American football's biggest game, the Super Bowl, is watched on US TV by nearly 100 million people. American football grew out of the sport of rugby, which was invented in the UK in the early 19th century. Both American football and rugby use an oval-shaped ball. When the ball hits the ground, its odd shape means that it can bounce in any direction.

To play American football or rugby, you need to be strong or fast – better still if you are both. American football is played in other parts of the world, too, including Japan, Mexico and Europe.

Ripley explains...

NFL players have had to wear helmets to protect their head since the 1940s.

Shoulder pads are made of shock absorbing foam with a hard plastic cover. These protect the players and also make them look much bigger than they really are!

Plastic knee pads fit into pockets inside the football trousers. They protect the players' knees when they crash to the ground.

ROUGH AND TUMBLE

American football is fun and fast but also very physical with a lot of body contact. Around 40,000 high-school players suffer concussion (a mild head injury) every year playing football. Quarterbacks or running backs, who are tackled most often, rarely get through a season without being injured.

SCHOOLBOY ERROR

Rugby began in 1823 when William Webb Ellis, a student at Rugby School in England, caught the ball during a game of football and ran towards the other team's goal. It is now played in over 100 countries worldwide.

Oooooofff!

GRRRRR

<<THE FRIDGE>>

William Perry, a popular defensive lineman for the Chicago Bears, was known as 'The Fridge' because of his 1.88-m, 173-kg square body. Yet at high school he could leap high enough to dunk a basketball!

twist it!

END ZONE

David Withoft, a young Green Bay Packers' fan, was so excited by his 2003 Christmas gift – a Packers' jersey with Brett Favre's No 4 – that he wore it every day for over four years.

The boys' American football team at De La Salle High School, Concord, California, won 151 games in a row from 1992 to 2004.

Willie McQueen was a great defence tackler for Flint Southwestern Academy High School team, Michigan, despite being only 0.9 m tall. He had been left with no legs after a railway accident.

Jim Purol of California sat in all 92,542 seats at the Pasadena Rose Bowl over a period of five days in 2008. He sat for 12 hours each day and took a cushion to stop him from getting a sore behind.

American footballer Roy Riegels became famous for running the wrong way! When playing for the California Golden Bears in the 1929 Rose Bowl, he picked up a fumble, lost his sense of direction, and ran 70 yards towards his own end zone. He was finally grabbed by one of his team-mates on his own one-yard line.

FASCINATING FACT! FASCINATING FACT!

The French national rugby team have a live cockerel as their mascot. Sometimes he even attends the team's training sessions. It gives them something to crow about!

Rooster booster

PEDAL POWER

Wheels can have up to 48 spokes to help deal with bumpy landings.

Riders can pedal forwards and backwards for tricks.

The handlebars can spin in a circle.

BMX magic

BMX (Bicycle Motocross) began in southern California in the 1970s, but is so popular that in 2008 it became an Olympic sport. The bikes are designed for performing tricks and for racing on hilly dirt tracks. Riders must wear a full-face helmet, elbow pads, knee pads and shin guards. Yet even the best riders sometimes get hurt. American Mat Hoffman has had over 50 operations and 500 stitches, and broken almost every bone in his body.

There are so many different sports you can do on a bike. Racing cyclists zoom around a track at nearly 80 km/h. Cyclo-cross competitors ride through woods and across such rough land that they have to get off and carry their bikes up steep hills. BMX bikers are able to perform fantastic jumps and acrobatic twists in mid-air. In 2008, Kevin Robinson of the USA soared 8.2 m into the air on a BMX bike – equal to jumping over a three-storey building.

There are endurance races, too. At the Lotoja race in the USA, riders cover 330 km in a single day. Other people ride bikes down glaciers and mountains, and even ride them backwards – sometimes playing a musical instrument at the same time!

ROUND AND ROUND

Austrian Marcus Stoeckl rode a mountain bike down a snow-covered mountain in Chile, reaching a speed of 210 km/h.

At the Down the Hill bike race in Taxco, Mexico, competitors ride mountain bikes through a house! They go in through a door, ride down a flight of stairs, and exit through another door.

Jumping from a ramp, Australian Nathan Rennie cleared over 36 m on his mountain bike in 2005.

At the 2009 X Games in Los Angeles, Anthony Napolitan performed two complete somersaults in mid-air to land the first-ever double front flip on a bicycle.

During the 1904 Tour de France – the world's most famous cycle race – French spectators sprinkled broken glass on the road so that the leaders would get punctures and allow their local favourite to win.

twist it!

Balancing act

Ripley explains...

When you pedal a bike, you use your muscles to create a force. You are like the engine for your bike. Bicycles are so efficient they can convert 80 per cent of the energy you supply at the pedals into energy that powers you along. To compare, a car engine converts only 25 per cent of the energy in petrol into useful power.

It's scary enough riding a bike around volcano craters or on cliff tops, but Canada's Kris Holm does it on a unicycle! The one-wheeled daredevil has ridden on the rail of a 60-m-high bridge, the edge of a 805-m-high cliff, and within 10 m of red-hot, bubbling lava on a volcano in Hawaii.

COASTING ALONG

With an oxygen tank on his back, Maaruf Bitar of Lebanon practises his favourite hobby – underwater cycling – off the coast of the Mediterranean city of Sidon. Underwater cyclists have ridden at depths of over 60 m beneath the sea, that's 30 times the depth of an Olympic swimming pool.

EXTREME ACTION

NO LIMITS

Who would think you could play Scrabble underwater or iron a T-shirt at the top of a mountain? You can, thanks to a new range of extreme sports designed to make gentle pursuits or boring jobs much more exciting.

Instead of doing their ironing in the living room, some people do it in caves, in a canoe, on top of a statue, in the middle of a forest, or while snowboarding. It has become so popular that now you can even play Wii extreme ironing – back in your living room!

If only Jim were as keen to iron at home!

Ironing on the roof of a car, Sahara Desert

Extreme housework! Sahara Desert

Don't look down!

Extremely silly

Extreme ironing was thought up by Englishman Phil Shaw in the 1990s and became so popular that the first Extreme Ironing World Championships took place in Germany in 2002. Eighty competitors from ten countries had to think up peculiar places for doing the ironing.

Cliff ironing – not for the faint hearted

Underwater ironing – poor results

Mountain ironing (note the use of crossed skis for an ironing board)

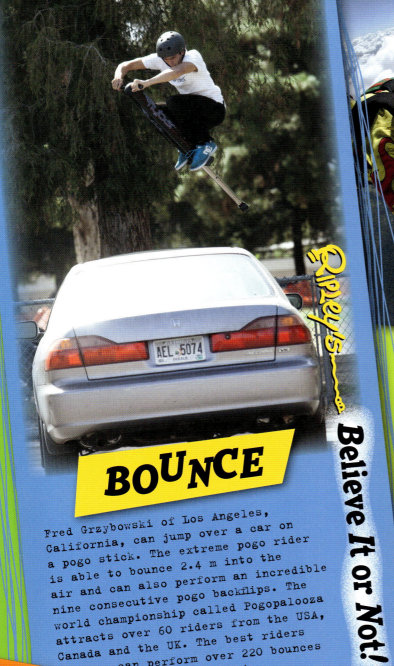

BOUNCE

Fred Grzybowski of Los Angeles, California, can jump over a car on a pogo stick. The extreme pogo rider is able to bounce 2.4 m into the air and can also perform an incredible nine consecutive pogo backflips. The world championship called Pogopalooza attracts over 60 riders from the USA, Canada and the UK. The best riders can perform over 220 bounces in a minute.

INSANE IRONING

- Two South Africans ironed while hanging from a rope across a 30-m-wide mountain gorge.
- A British pair did some ironing at a height of 5,425 m on Mount Everest.
- In 2007, Henry Cookson dragged his iron and ironing board 1,770 km across the frozen wastes of Antarctica.
- Australian Robert Fry threw himself off the side of a cliff in the Blue Mountains with an iron, a board, some laundry and a parachute!
- In 2009, 86 British scuba divers ironed underwater at the same time – in water as cold as -2°C.

EXTREME SCRABBLE

To celebrate the 60th anniversary of Scrabble in 2008, extreme enthusiasts played in some crazy places. Skydivers Nicole Angelides and Ramsey Kent played Scrabble at 4,000 m above Florida. With each move, they had to glue the tiles to the board to stop them blowing away.

twist it!

ABOVE AND BEYOND

American Peter Jenkins has started a new sport – extreme tree climbing. He and his friends climb trees and perform acrobatic stunts. These include balancing on the branches and running across the canopy (the top) of the trees. They also tree surf, where they go high into the tree on a windy day and ride the branches like waves.

On a 2006 tour, extreme cello players Clare Wallace, Jeremy Dawson and James Rees carried their musical instruments on to the roofs of 31 different cathedrals in England and played a short concert on each.

In 2008, while orbiting in the International Space Station at 8 km a second, Canadian astronaut Greg Chamitoff played a game of extreme chess against a team of US students on Earth.

Running wild

Free running, or parkour, is a form of urban acrobatics. You run through towns and cities, vaulting walls and railings as stylishly as possible, adding spins or twists in mid-air. You can use ledges, handrails or steps to perform handstands and somersaults. You just make it up as you go along.

SHOW SOME MUSCLE

BODY POWER

Some people can do amazing things with their body. They can squeeze it through the head of a tennis racquet – with the strings taken out, of course. They can balance on their head on a high wire just a couple of centimetres wide, thousands of metres up in the air without a safety net.

Back on the ground, in 1980 a Japanese man did more than 10,000 push-ups nonstop, and free-running experts can jump between the roofs of buildings, just like in the movies.

IN A SPIN

Kareena Oates from Australia is able to rotate 100 hula hoops around her body at the same time. She has also spun 41 hula hoops around her waist while suspended in the air by her wrists.

UP, UP, UP...

At the Tarragona Castells festival in Spain, acrobats climb over each other to form amazing human towers. There have been as many as ten levels of people standing on each other's shoulders, but sometimes the whole thing just comes crashing down.

ENERGY BUZZ

American Don Claps can perform more than 1,200 consecutive cartwheels, and he can even carry on doing them while drinking water from a paper cup!

In 2009, Davit Fahradyan of Armenia completed 354 arm-aching turns on a horizontal bar.

New Yorker Ashrita Furman hula hooped underwater for 2 minutes 20 seconds at a Florida dolphin centre in 2007. He used a special metal hoop and was able to breathe air through scuba-diving equipment.

Olga Berberich completed 251 jumps with a rope in just one minute in Germany in 2007.

Contortionist Daniel Browning-Smith, of Los Angeles, California, is so flexible he can squeeze his entire body into a box the size of a microwave oven.

Working in shifts of two people at a time, eight boys, aged between eight and 11, bounced nonstop on an inflatable castle in Michigan for 24 hours in 2008.

HUMAN FLAG

Canadian gymnast and acrobat Dominic Lacasse held himself horizontally on a bar as a 'Human Flag', for 39 seconds, a display of incredible strength.

twist it!

GET YOUR SKATES ON

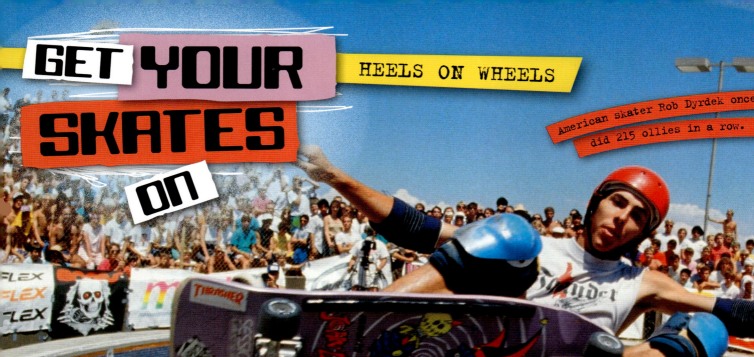

American skater Rob Dyrdek once did 215 ollies in a row.

In 2006, Welshman Dave Cornthwaite spent 90 days on a skateboard, riding it all the way across Australia – a distance of more than 5,600 km! Skateboarders love to try new challenges. One man jumped over four cars on a skateboard, and another built a skateboard so big that nearly 30 people could stand on it at the same time.

Dude!

The ollie is one of the most popular aerial skating tricks. You bend down, push your back foot down on the tail end of the board and then allow the board to pop back up. As you leap into the air, the board appears to be stuck to your feet, as if by magic.

There are now more than 18 million skateboarders in the world. You could also try roller hockey, speed skating, or if you can really stretch your arms and legs, the latest Indian craze of limbo skating!

GREAT SKATES

Skateboarding was born when Californian surfers wanted something to surf on when the waves in the sea were flat. Believe it or not, top skaters have reached speeds of nearly 100 km/h.

DANNY'S WAY

In Mexico City in 2006, American skater Danny Way landed a sensational backflip, which he called El Camino ('The Way'). He sped down a 23-m-high ramp and leaped 21 m through the air at a speed of 80 km/h. The previous year he had jumped over the Great Wall of China on a skateboard. Not bad for someone who says he is afraid of heights!

Roller skates first became popular in the 1880s.

The lowdown

Limbo skaters have to be strong and flexible to skate under more than 50 parked cars at a time. They practise for months to get their body into the right position. Young limbo skater Aniket Chindak can roller-skate under cars that are just 24 cm off the ground.

TURNING HEADS

At the 1999 X Games, American Tony Hawk became the first skater to land a 900: that's 2½ rotations in mid-air.

Bingo, a Border collie, used to ride through the streets of Winnipeg, Canada, on a skateboard picking up litter.

In 2000, Richie Carrasco completed 142 dizzying 360-degree spins on a skateboard without stopping.

A roller skate invented by Frenchman M Mercier in the 1900s was powered by a two-cylinder petrol engine. This enabled the skater to zoom along at speeds of 30 km/h.

Around 280 roller skaters held on to the waist of the person in front of them to form a giant skating chain that snaked through the streets of Singapore City in 2006.

Rohan Ajit Kokane is so good at limbo skating he can do it under cars while blindfolded!

twist it!

SPEED SKATER

German inline skater Dirk Auer reached incredible speeds of nearly 300 km/h while being dragged behind a high-powered motorbike. Dirk is used to extreme skating and has also managed to skate along the roof of an airborne plane and down a rollercoaster.

Ripley's Believe It or Not!

ROLLER MAN

Frenchman Jean-Yves Blondeau wears a special plastic suit with sets of rollers attached. It means he can roll down the motorway at nearly 100 km/h. He can even overtake motorbikes!

GOAL CRAZY

FANTASTIC FOOTBALL

About 3.5 billion people either play or watch football, making it the world's most popular sport. Every country plays the game, right down to tiny islands. On the Isles of Scilly, off the southwest coast of England, the league is made up of just two teams who play each other every week! It does mean the draw for the cup is not very exciting...

Football is fast and skilful. Some people love the game so much they name their children after their favourite players, dye their hair in their team's colours, or travel thousands of miles just to watch their team. The best players are treated like superstars and are paid over £100,000 a week. Boys and girls play football, but you need to be fit to be a professional, as some top players run up to 10 km during a match.

GOAL CRAZY

Freezing Footie

Jungfrau Mountain — Switzerland

International footballers staged a 2007 exhibition match on an artificial pitch laid out on a glacier. It took place in the shadow of Switzerland's 4,160-m Jungfrau Mountain. The high-altitude air was so tiring that the teams played just five minutes each half.

Dan Magness — Britain

Using his feet, thighs, chest and head, Britain's Dan Magness kept a football in the air for 24 hours. He touched the ball around 250,000 times, knowing that the smallest lapse in concentration would mean he would have to start all over again!

FREE KICKS

Some football matches are decided by penalty shoot-outs, where eight kicks are often enough to get a result. At the end of a 2005 Namibian Cup tie in Africa, the penalty contest went on for an incredible 48 kicks and lasted nearly an hour!

Important football matches often attract crowds of over 70,000 people, but the 1950 World Cup final between Brazil and Uruguay was watched by nearly 200,000 spectators.

An annual football match called the Calcio takes place in Florence, Italy, between two teams of 27 players dressed in 16th-century costume. It is a rough game, and players are allowed to elbow, kick, and even head butt each other!

Welsh footie fan Steve Thatcher named his son after all the players in his favourite team, Cardiff City. It means young Sam has 12 middle names!

twist it!

GOAL CRAZY

GOOOAAALLL!!!

Nani — Portugal

Portuguese football star Nani performs his famous backflip celebration after scoring a goal for Manchester United. The fans love it – as long as he doesn't injure himself doing it.

GOAL CRAZY

Tiny Field — Microscopic

Created by technology, this football pitch is so tiny that 20,000 of them could fit on the tip of a single human hair. It has all the markings of a full-sized pitch but can only be viewed using a really powerful microscope.

GOAL CRAZY

The Legendary Pelé

Pelé — Brazil

The great Brazilian footballer Pelé scored 1,281 goals in his career – more than any other professional player. He helped his country to win the World Cup three times, and scored the opening goal in the 1970 final when Brazil beat Italy 4–1.

GOAL CRAZY

Brainy Ball

Adidas — Germany

Adidas has designed a clever football. It contains a chip that sends a radio signal to the referee's watch in less than a second of the ball crossing the goal line. So there should be no more arguments about whether or not a shot was a goal.

GOAL CRAZY

On the Head

Manoj Mishra — India

Indian footie fan Manoj Mishra won a competition by balancing a ball on his head for 14 hours. He practised yoga exercises so that he could get used to keeping still for so long. Afterwards he dedicated his success to his hero, Argentinian football legend Diego Maradona.

FLYING HIGH

TAKING TO THE SKIES

Many humans love to fly. As we don't have wings like a bird, we try the next best thing and take up sports such as hang gliding, paragliding, ballooning, gliding and skydiving. American skydiver Don Kellner has made over 36,000 jumps, and Jay Stokes once made 640 jumps in a single day! Skydivers free fall at 200 km/h before the safety parachute opens and they descend gently to the ground.

If you are worried about heights, you don't have to go up alone. You could always take your dog with you. Brutus, a miniature dachshund from California, made more than 70 jumps with his owner!

Mike Howard, an airline pilot, walked along a 5.8-m-long pole from one balloon to another, 1,200 m above the USA, in 2004. When he had completed the daring tightrope walk, he parachuted to the ground.

YEEE-HAAAA..."

Although skydiving looks dangerous, in the USA there is only one death for every 100,000 jumps.

JUMP!

Skydivers jump from airplanes, helicopters and even hot-air balloons. Once their parachutes are open, they control their direction by pulling toggles on the end of steering lines attached to the chute. That's how they can land on a small cross marked on the ground after jumping from 4,000 m.

WAA-HOOOO...

Ripley's Believe It or Not!

Buddy the Labrador and his owner, Bill Kimball of San Diego, California, went hang gliding together for more than eight years. Buddy joined Bill on over 75 flights.

twist it!

In Japan they stage kite fights. Competing teams tie sharp razor blades and broken glass to the tail strings of their kites and fly them against one another. The aim is to rip the opposing kite to shreds so that it can no longer fly.

In just eight days, Englishman Martin Downs skydived on six continents: Africa, Europe, South America, North America, Australia and Asia.

Vijaypat Singhania flew a hot-air balloon to an incredible altitude of 21,027 m over India in 2005.

In 2004, Bob Holloway flew 4,152 km in a powered paraglider from Astoria, Oregon, to Washington, Missouri.

Holly Budge from England skydived over Mount Everest in 2008. She jumped from a plane at 8,990 m and reached speeds of 225 km/h and braved temperatures of −40°C.

SUPERFLY GUYS

Ripley explains...

Sail

Rigging

Harness

Control Bar

Hang gliders can stay thousands of metres in the air for hours, soaring through the skies like an eagle. A hang glider has a lightweight aluminium frame, a big nylon wing, and no engine. The pilot is attached to the frame by a harness. There are no switches or buttons to worry about. Pilots steer by shifting their body weight on the frame, then all they have to do is relax and admire the views.

<<human bird>>

American Jeb Corliss comes as close as any human has to flying. Wearing a special winged jumpsuit, he takes part in the scary sport of proximity wingsuit flying. He jumps from a helicopter or off a cliff edge thousands of metres up and flies terrifyingly close to mountain faces. Jeb once flew down the 4,478-m-high Matterhorn Mountain in Switzerland, within just 1.5 m of the jagged cliff-face, and reached speeds of 160 km/h.

SURF'S UP
RIDING THE WAVES

It's not only waves that are a danger to surfers. Each year as many as 80 surfers are attacked by sharks.

Ripley explains...

You catch a wave by pushing the water towards the back of the surfboard with your hands, moving you forwards. As you ride on the wave the water rises beneath you and pushes you forwards faster and faster. All the time gravity is trying to push you down, while buoyancy is pushing you up.

84 surfers rode the same wave at the same time off the coast of Brazil in 2007.

Have you ever wished you could ride a wave on a surfboard? Some waves are huge – over 20 m high. That's more than four times the height of an adult giraffe! That just makes it even more of a challenge for a surfer. You can surf a wave standing up, crouching or lying down – and some surfers have managed to stay on the same wave for half an hour. There are no rules, you just do what you enjoy.

The first surfers – in Tahiti in the 18th century – used planks of wood, but today's surfboards are made of lightweight polyurethane foam. Surfing is really popular in places like California, Florida and Hawaii, where the shape of the seabed and strong winds create big waves.

34

RIDING HIGH

Kite surfers use wind power to help them speed across the water and soar up to 50 m in the air. They stand on a board and hold on to a large controllable kite. The aim is to do tricks such as jumps, spins and even somersaults, and to see how high and long they can jump off waves.

SAY WHAT?

CATCH A WAVE

This is when you launch yourself into the path of a suitable wave.

Kite surfers can go great distances when the wind is behind them. In 2006, UK kite surfer Kirsty Jones travelled 225 km from Lanzarote in the Canary Islands to Morocco.

Donald 'DJ' Dettloff has created a colourful fence from more than 700 surfboards near his home in Hawaii.

PLAIN SAILING

Windsurfers attach a sail to their surfboards. When the wind blows into the sail from behind, it makes the board go faster: sometimes up to 100 km/h! Windsurfers can perform amazing stunts, jumps and spins.

Ripley's Believe It or Not!®

In California they have a surfing contest that's just for dogs. Four-legged surfing dudes show their style on their own and with human partners. The winner receives a basket full of dog treats.

FASCINATING FACT! FASCINATING FACT!

IN THE RUNNING

MARATHONS

People can't run as fast as cheetahs, but they can run much further. They need great stamina to do this. The longest running race in the Olympics is the marathon at just over 26 miles (42 km).

Just running a marathon is exhausting, but some athletes need greater challenges. So they run extreme (ultra) marathons that are a mega 160 km long. Occasionally, someone will even run all the way around the world – with lots of stops, of course!

The first marathon

In 490BC, Pheidippides, a Greek soldier, ran about 25 miles (40 km) from the town of Marathon to Athens to announce that the Greeks had defeated the invading Persians in battle. The route was exhausting, and shortly after arriving in Athens Pheidippides fell to the ground dead.

In 1896, the first modern Olympic Games in Athens held a race of roughly the same length in his honour. It became known as the marathon.

MARATHON FACT FILE

- More than **400,000 people** in the USA compete in marathons annually.
- More than **800 marathons** are run in the world each year. The biggest marathons can have tens of thousands of runners.
- A marathon runner will go through **two pairs of trainers** while training for the race.
- Top marathon athletes will run **160 km** a week in training.
- It takes the average woman **51,214 steps** to complete a marathon.
- In 2008, 64-year-old Texan Larry Macon ran **105 marathons.**

Sand marathon

A competitor climbs a sand dune during the 2009 Marathon des Sables in the Sahara Desert. This desert marathon is considered the hardest in the world.

COOL RUNNING

Runners tackle rough mountain trails in the 2006 Everest Marathon. The starting line is at 5,180 m near Mount Everest Base Camp in Nepal, making it the highest marathon in the world.

Bringing up the rear >>

Englishman Lloyd Scott walked the 2002 New York and London marathons wearing a 55-kg antique diving suit. In London, it took him five days and eight hours. In 2003, he wore the same suit to complete a marathon underwater!

HAVING A BALL

There are many ways to complete a marathon. This man at the 2008 Berlin Marathon was running in a sphere!

STAYING POWER

Dave Heeley from England ran seven marathons on seven continents in seven days in 2008, even though he is blind.

Michal Kapral, from Toronto, Canada, ran a marathon in 3 hours 7 minutes in 2005 while juggling three balls at the same time.

Between 1997 and 2003, England's Robert Garside ran 48,000 km around the world in 2,062 days.

US soldier Jake Truex ran 5,000 m in just over 22 minutes in Germany in 2006 with a heavy 18-kg backpack strapped to his back.

Charlie Engle (USA), Ray Zahab (Canada) and Kevin Lin (Taiwan) ran the same distance as two marathons a day for 111 days to cross the 6,400-km Sahara Desert on foot in 2007. They had to cope with temperatures that were over 37°C by day, but below freezing at night.

DID YOU KNOW?

At the London Marathon...

They use 710,000 bottles of water, 950 portable toilets, 500 stretchers and 68 ambulances.

The blue paint that marks out the course is steam-cleaned off as the last runner passes, so the streets of London can be quickly returned to normal.

Australia's Kurt Fearnley completed the 2009 race in a wheelchair in a record 1 hour 28 minutes 56 seconds.

The London Marathon was the first to be run over 26.2 miles. This is because at the 1908 Olympics the Royal Box lay 385 yards (350 m) beyond the 26-mile finish line. The race was extended so it could finish beneath the Royal Box.

RISKY BUSINESS

Over the past 30 years, dozens of dangerous sports have been introduced that are exciting to do but, when things go wrong, can result in serious injury, even death. Only really physically fit people should attempt these sports – and even then they must have the right equipment, or the consequences could be fatal.

Cave divers plunge to depths of up to 30 m underwater in total darkness at the risk of losing their way or running out of air. Kayakers ride over the world's highest waterfalls, hitting terrifying speeds of 110 km/h on the way down. Bungee jumpers leap from bridges high above raging rivers with one end of an elastic cord tied to their ankles and the other end tied to the jumping-off point. For some people sport is only fun if they are putting their life at risk.

In the balance

This is not a trick photo. Eskil Ronningsbakken really is performing a one-handed handstand while balancing on the edge of a ladder attached to a 300-m-high cliff in Norway. He was able to do this by adding 150 kg of weights at the balancing end. It still looks pretty scary though.

SAY WHAT?

BASE JUMPING

BASE jumping is named after the places you jump from: Buildings (skyscrapers, statues), Antennas (radio masts, cranes), Spans (bridges), and Earth (cliffs).

DEATH DEFYING

READY TO ROLL

Have you ever wondered what it is like to be a hamster in a wheel? Well, the sport of Zorbing lets you find out. Zorbonauts roll down hills inside large transparent plastic spheres, reaching speeds of over 50 km/h.

CRAZY KAYAKING

One of the world's top extreme kayakers is fearless Jesse Combs from Oregon. Jesse risks life and limb by taking his kayak over steep crashing waterfalls such as this 20-m drop at the Mesa Falls in Idaho.

A NEED FOR SPEED

David Kirke, founder of England's Dangerous Sports Club, adapted a medieval rock-throwing device called a trebuchet so that humans could be catapulted 17 m into the air in under two seconds.

Bull running takes place in several Spanish towns, most famously in Pamplona. Participants have to run in front of a herd of angry bulls that have been let loose in the streets. Fifteen people have been killed in the Pamplona event since 1910.

Tyler Bradt paddled a kayak down the raging waters of the 33-m Alexandra Falls in Canada, and didn't flip once.

In 1991, John Kockelman made a bungee jump of 300 m from a hot-air balloon 1,500 m above California.

In BASE jumping, people hurl themselves from tall structures with just a parachute to save them from certain death. The thrill is to wait as long as possible before pulling the parachute cord. Here, leaping 280 m from the Menara Kuala Lumpur Tower in Malaysia, this jumper will have six seconds of freefall before he has to use his parachute.

People have **BASE jumped** from San Francisco's Golden Gate Bridge, the Eiffel Tower in Paris and New York City's Empire State Building.

In 2006, Australians Glenn Singleman and Heather Swan jumped off a **6,500-m-high** precipice on Meru Peak, India, and landed on a 5,000-m-high glacier.

In 2006, Dan Schilling made **201 BASE jumps** in 24 hours off a bridge 14 m above the Snake River Canyon, Idaho. He kept jumping even after fracturing his wrist.

An average of **15 people** are killed while BASE jumping every year.

TWIST IT!

HAVING A BALL

Believe it or not, golf was the first sport to be played on the Moon. Astronaut Alan Shepard hit a couple of shots on the 1971 *Apollo 14* Moon mission. Ball games such as golf, bowling, pool and table tennis are played all over the world. Baseball also has a wide following, and an amazing 42 million people play it in the USA alone. Cricket is played in the UK, Australia, South Africa and Asia.

Most of these sports are over 100 years old, and some have their origins in ancient history. A form of bowling was played in Egypt as far back as 3200BC. The game was outlawed in England in 1366 because King Edward III wanted his soldiers to concentrate on archery practice instead.

The odds of a spectator being hit by a ball at a Major League game are 300,000 to 1.

Nearly 80 million people pay to watch Major League baseball in a season.

Big teams like the New York Yankees average attendances of over 50,000 per game.

The athletic Nomar Garciaparra first starred for the Boston Red Sox in the 1990s. He is one of only a handful of players in Major League baseball history to have hit two grand slams (a home run hit when there are runners at three bases) during a single game.

UPSCALE BALL

Instead of being covered in leather, this cricket ball is covered in 2,704 diamonds. Made in Sri Lanka, it is said to be the first life-sized diamond-and-gold cricket ball in the world.

CRICKET ODDITIES

- Cricket is played by two teams of 11 players. One team bowls and fields while the other bats. A team is in (at bat) until ten of its batsmen are out. Then the other team is in!

- Batsmen try to score runs by hitting the ball a long way. If a batsman is out for no runs, he has scored a duck — because zero is shaped like a duck's egg.

- The bowlers aim at three wooden stumps in the ground known as the wicket. They take it in turn to bowl 'overs', which consist of bowling six balls at the batsman. If no runs are scored off an over, it is called a maiden.

- There are ten ways a batsman can be out, including bowled, caught and leg before wicket (lbw).

twist it!

Every Thanksgiving, Cincinnati, Ohio, hosts a Turkey Bowl, where competitors bowl frozen turkeys instead of bowling balls!

Playing baseball for Portsmouth High School, Ohio, in 2008, triplets Howard, John and Matt Harcha all hit home runs, in the order of their birth from oldest to youngest.

In 2007, English golfer David Huggins hit his third hole-in-one...and he was only eight years old.

Table tennis was first played in Victorian England in the 1880s on a dining room table, often using a cigar box lid as a bat, a champagne cork as a ball, and a row of books as a net!

PLAY BALL

English golfer Andrew Winfield teed off from the summit of Africa's Mount Kilimanjaro in 2008, 5,895 m above sea level.

BILLION-DOLLAR MAN

American golfer Tiger Woods became the first ever athlete to earn a billion dollars. He has won more than 70 tour events and when he was only three years old he shot an amazing score of 48 over nine holes at a golf club in California. He usually wears a red shirt on the final round of tournaments because he believes it helps him to win.

Perfect pitch

Jim Abbott was a Major League baseball pitcher in the 1990s even though he was born with only one hand. In 1993, playing for the New York Yankees, he even pitched a no-hitter (where the opposing team has no hits in an entire game) against the Cleveland Indians. This was a fantastic achievement because on average just two no-hitters a year have been thrown in Major League baseball since 1875.

WACKY RACES

FUN RUNS

You don't need an engine to take part in a wacky race, just a daft sense of humour. In various places across the world people push, pull or carry beds, toilets, coffins, even their wives – all in the name of sport.

For serious athletes who like a fun run, there is the mad dash up the stairs of the Empire State Building in New York. Germany's Thomas Dold won in 2006, 2007, 2008 and 2009, and he also excels at another crazy form of racing – running backwards!

BIRDS IN FLIGHT

Lightweight jockeys ride ostriches in a race in Shanghai, China. Ostrich racing is also popular in South Africa and in several locations in the USA. Ostriches can run at 72 km/h, the fastest running speed of any bird. Ostriches are harder to steer than horses, so although the jockeys have special saddles and reins, they still regularly fall off.

STEP UP THE PACE

Each year more than 300 runners take part in the race up the stairs of the Empire State Building. The climb to the observation deck is up 320 m, 86 floors, and 1,576 stairs. It takes most of the runners about 15 minutes to reach the observation deck. The building's elevator can get there in less than a minute.

DEAD FUNNY

Every year in Manitou Springs, Colorado, teams race coffins with a living female occupant. Around 40 coffins take part. They are rerunning the legend of Emma Crawford, who died in 1890 and was buried on top of Red Mountain, only to have her coffin slide down the canyon in 1929 after heavy rains.

Quackers!

More than 200,000 blue plastic ducks floated nearly a kilometre downstream on the River Thames in the 2009 Great British Duck Race. Each duck had a number, and people picked a duck, hoping that theirs would be the first to reach the finish and win them a cash prize.

IN IT TO WIN IT

People race decorated outdoor toilets through the streets of Dawson City in Canada! For the Great Klondike Outhouse Race, teams speed around a 2.4 km course. One person has to sit on the toilet the whole time!

In Sydney, Australia, there is a race solely for women wearing high stiletto-heeled shoes. The trick is to get to the finish line without spraining your ankle.

There's a Grand Prix in France that's just for homemade pedal cars. Drivers pump their legs around Valentigney for up to three hours, but design is just as important as speed. That's why you might see a man in a monkey mask driving a banana-shaped car!

How about doing the 100 m...on stilts? In the Philippines, competitors perch on top of 1.8-m stilts made of bamboo and walk along the course as fast as they can.

Marry and carry

Estonia's Madis Uusorg carries his wife Inga Klausen to victory in the 2007 Wife-carrying World Championships in Finland. The race is run over an obstacle course and the winner receives his wife's weight in beer.

¡TWIST IT!

FUN AND GAMES

The Olympic Games are the greatest sporting show on earth. The ancient Olympics were held in Greece starting in the 8th century BC – nearly 3,000 years ago. Sports included the javelin, long jump, running in armour, and even kissing! After a long break, the Olympics were brought back in 1896 and are now held every four years. An incredible 27 million people watched the 2012 Olympics in London, UK, either on TV or online.

In London, more than 10,490 athletes from 204 countries competed in more than 302 events, from athletics to wrestling. The Winter Olympics are just as exciting, featuring sports such as skiing, ice skating and bobsled. The winner of each event receives a gold medal, second place gets a silver medal and third place gets a bronze medal. These are the most important prizes in sport.

STEVE REDGRAVE

A powerful rower, Britain's Steve Redgrave (second from left) in 2000 was one of only four Olympians to have won a gold medal at five consecutive Olympic Games.

Fan-tastic

To celebrate the 2008 Olympics in Beijing, a Chinese man, Dr. Wei Sheng, pierced his head, face, hands and chest with 2,008 needles in the five colours of the Olympic rings.

EDWIN MOSES

Edwin Moses of the USA won gold in the 400 metres hurdles at both the 1976 and 1984 Olympics. Between 1977 and 1987 he was undefeated, winning a record 122 consecutive races.

4,200 athletes from 170 countries took part in the 2012 Paralympics. These Games are for athletes with a physical disability or vision impairment. Sports include wheelchair basketball and wheelchair tennis.

US swimmer Michael Phelps won eight gold medals at the 2008 Beijing Olympics. It was the first time that this had been achieved by a competitor at a single Olympic Games.

FASCINATING FACT! FASCINATING FACT!

Live pigeon shooting was an event at the 1900 Olympics. Nearly 300 birds were killed. It was the first and only time in Olympic history that animals were killed on purpose.

twist it!

GOING FOR GOLD

At the 1904 Olympics, George Eyser (USA) won six gymnastics medals, including three gold, despite having a wooden left leg.

Women were not allowed to compete in track and field events at the Olympics until 1928. However, so many collapsed at the end of the 800 metres in that year that the event was banned until 1960.

A 1956 Olympic water-polo match between Hungary and the USSR (modern-day Russia) was abandoned after the teams started fighting underwater.

After winning a rowing gold medal at the 1956 Olympics, 18-year-old Russian Vyacheslav Ivanov quickly lost it. He threw the medal into the air in celebration, but it landed in the lake. He dived in but was unable to find it.

The USA are the reigning Olympic rugby champions. That's because rugby was last featured in the Olympics in 1924 when the USA beat France 17–3 in the final.

Party time

The opening ceremony at the 2012 London Olympics was watched by 62,000 people in the stadium and 27 million worldwide. The ceremony, called 'Isles of Wonder', cost £27 million and lasted for four hours.

CLARA HUGHES

Canada's Clara Hughes is one of only a few athletes to win medals at both the Summer and Winter Olympics. She succeeded at both cycling and speed skating.

MICHAEL PHELPS

SPORTS INDEX

Bold numbers refer to main entries; numbers in *italic* refer to the illustrations

ACKNOWLEDGEMENTS

COVER (t/l) © Speedfighter – Fotolia.com, (c) © Diego Cervo – Fotolia.com, (c/l) © Feng Yu – Fotolia.com, (t) © Albo – Fotolia.com, (b/r) www.jw-sportfoto.de; **2** (b) Reuters/Claro Cortes, (t) Anja Niedringhaus/AP/Press Association Images; **3** Georges Christen; **4** (b/l) © Michael Lawlor – Fotolia.com, (b/c) © kamphi – Fotolia.com, (t) iStock.com, (b/r) © Terry Morris – Fotolia.com; **5** (t/r) © Thomas Lammeyer – iStock.com, (b/l) © Michael Lawlor – Fotolia.com, (b/cl, b/c, b/cr) N & B – Fotolia.com, (b/r) Pawel Nowik – Fotolia.com, (r) © Feng Yu – Fotolia.com; **6** (b/l) Reuters/United Photos; **6–7** (dp) Reuters/Stringer USA; **7** (r) Anja Niedringhaus/AP/Press Association Images; **8** Reuters/Stefano Rellandini; **9** (t/l) Reuters/Fahad Shadeed, (b/r) Reuters/Claro Cortes, (b) Reuters/Chaiwat Subprasom; **10** (l) Phil Walter/Getty Images, (t/r, c) Michael Martin/Barcroft Media Ltd, (b/r) © Chepko Danil – iStock.com; **11** (r) John Chapple/Rex Features, (t/l) Tony Gentile/Reuters, (b/r) Reuters Photographer/Reuters; **12** William Tremblay wl_tremblay@hotmail.com; **13** (t/l) Archive Photos/Getty Images, (b/r) Georges Christen; **14** (b/r) Mike Hewitt/Getty Images; **14–15** (t) Nathaniel S. Butler/NBAE/Getty Images; **15** (b/l) © Thomas Lammeyer – iStock.com, (b/r) Toby Melville/Reuters, (c) David E. Klutho/Sports Illustrated/Getty Images; **16** (t) © Pierre Jacques/Hemis/Corbis, (b) Gary Caskey/Reuters; **17** (t/r) Reuters/Yuriko Nakao, (t/l) © Reuters/Corbis, (r) S Levy/Getty Images; **18** (l) Sam Yeh/AFP/Getty Images, (t/l) Reuters Photographer/Reuters; **18–19** Sam Yeh/AFP/Getty Images; **19** (t/l) Heribert Proepper/AP/Press Association Images, (b/r) © Julien Rousset – Fotolia.com; **20** (l) David Purdy/Landov/Press Association Images, (r) © George Peters – iStock.com; **20–21** (dp) © Peter Baxter – Fotolia.com; **21** (t/l) Lynne Cameron/PA Wire/Press Association Images, (l) Jonathan Daniel/Getty Images, (b/r) Damien Meyer/AFP/Getty Images; **22** Lester Lefkowitz/Corbis; **23** (l) seanwhite.net/Sean White Photography, (r) AFP/Getty Images; **24** (t/l, t/r, c, b, r) Rex Features; **25** (t/l) Barcroft Media via Getty Images, (t/r) Barcroft Media Ltd; **26** (t) © Maxym Boner – iStock.com, (l) © Arturo Limon – iStock.com, (b/r) © Bart Sadowski – iStock.com; **27** (l) Alfaqui/Barcroft Media Ltd, (t/r) Samantha Sin/AFP/Getty Images, (r) Ermann J. Knippertz/AP/Press Association Images; **28–29** (c) Doug Pensinger/Getty Images, (b) Anthony Acosta; **29** (b/l) www.jw-sportfoto.de, (b/r) ChinaFotoPress/Cheng Jiang/Photocome/Press Association Images, (t/r) © Simon de Trey-White/Barcroft Pacific; **30** (t/l) Reuters/Christian Hartmann, (c) Johnny Green/PA Wire/Press Association Images; **30–31** (dp) Stephen Pond/Empics Sport; **31** (t/l) Wenn, (t) Kin Cheung/AP/Press Association Images, (t/r) © Reuters/Corbis, (b/r) © EuroPics [CEN], (b/l) Rex Features; **32** © Daniel Ramsbott/epa/Corbis; **33** (b/l, b) © Axel Koester/Corbis, (t/l) Sam Barcroft/Rex Features, (r) © Daniel Cardiff – iStock.com; **34** Neale Haynes/Rex Features; **35** (l) Warren Bolster, (r) © Don Bayley – iStock.com, (b/l) Denis Poroy/AP/Press Association Images, (b/r) John Hugg: mauisurfboard.com; huggsmaui.com; **36** Pierre Verdy/Getty Images; **37** (l) Getty Images, (t) Reuters/Str New, (c) Reuters/Pawel Kopczynski; **38** (sp) Sindre Lundvold/Barcroft Media, (b/r) Sipa Press/Rex Features; **39** (l) Photograph by Darin Quoid, (t/r) © Jörg Hackemann – Fotolia.com; **40** (sp) Paul Spinelli/MLB Photos via Getty Images, (b/r) Sena Vidanagama/Stringer/Getty Images; **41** (t/r) iStock.com, (b/l) John Zich/AFP/Getty Images, (b/r) Dave Martin/AP/Press Association Images; **42** (b/l) Reuters/Brendan Mcdermid, (b/r) Andra DuRee Martin; **42–43** (t) Reuters/Nir Elias; **43** (l) Reuters/Lehtikuva Lehtikuva, (t/r) Jonathan Hordle/Rex Features, (t) © Michael Flippo – iStock.com; **44** ((b/l) Sipa Press/Rex Features, (c) ChinaFotoPress/Photocome/Press Association Images; **44–45** (dp) © Luc Santerre Castonguay – iStock.com, (t/r) Bob Jones/Rex Features; **45** (b) Reuters/Staff Photographer, (l) The World of Sports SC/Rex Features, (b/r) Reuters/Max Rossi

Key: t = top, b = bottom, c = centre, l = left, r = right, sp = single page, dp = double page, bgd = background

All other photos are from Ripley's Entertainment Inc. All artwork by Rocket Design (East Anglia) Ltd.

Every attempt has been made to acknowledge correctly and contact copyright holders and we apologise in advance for any unintentional errors or omissions, which will be corrected in future editions.

Ripley's HUMAN BODY

Believe It or Not!

PUBLISHING

a Jim Pattison Company

Written by Camilla de la Bedoyere
Consultant Dr. Irfan Ghani

PUBLISHING

Publisher Anne Marshall

Managing Editor Rebecca Miles
Picture Researcher James Proud
Editors Lisa Regan, Rosie Alexander
Assistant Editor Amy Harrison
Proofreader Judy Barratt
Indexer Hilary Bird

Art Director Sam South
Design Rocket Design (East Anglia) Ltd
Reprographics Stephan Davis

www.ripleys.com

PUBLISHER'S NOTE
While every effort has been made to verify the accuracy of the entries in this book, the Publishers cannot be held responsible for any errors contained in the work. They would be glad to receive any information from readers.

WARNING
Some of the stunts and activities in this book are undertaken by experts and should not be attempted by anyone without adequate training and supervision.

PAGE 8

Contents

TWISTS

PAGE 7

PAGE 37

PAGE 14

Body Beautiful

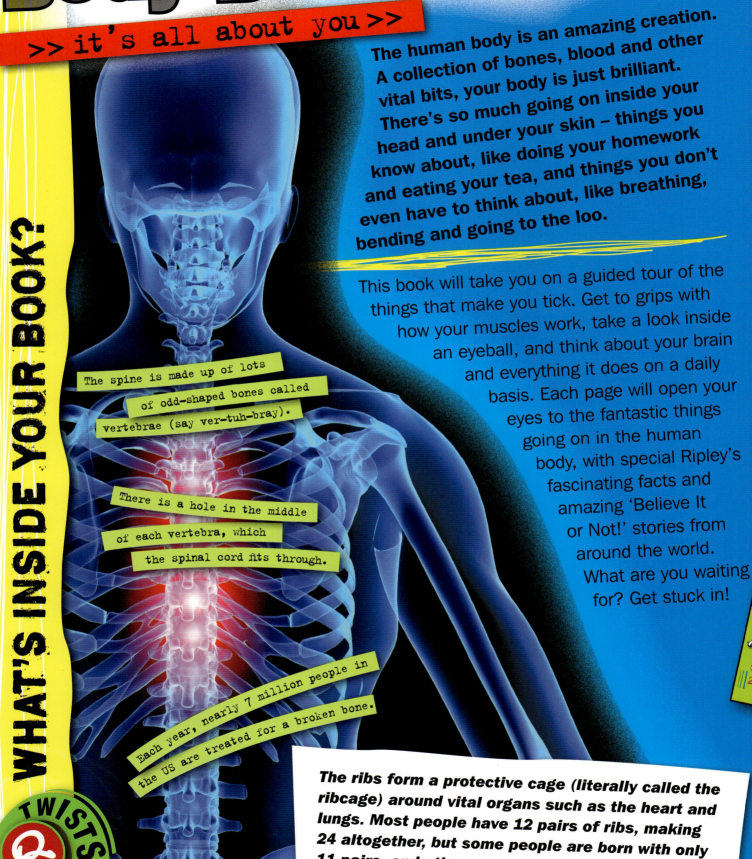

The human body is an amazing creation. A collection of bones, blood and other vital bits, your body is just brilliant. There's so much going on inside your head and under your skin – things you know about, like doing your homework and eating your tea, and things you don't even have to think about, like breathing, bending and going to the loo.

This book will take you on a guided tour of the things that make you tick. Get to grips with how your muscles work, take a look inside an eyeball, and think about your brain and everything it does on a daily basis. Each page will open your eyes to the fantastic things going on in the human body, with special Ripley's fascinating facts and amazing 'Believe It or Not!' stories from around the world. What are you waiting for? Get stuck in!

WHAT'S INSIDE YOUR BOOK?

The spine is made up of lots of odd-shaped bones called vertebrae (say ver-tuh-bray).

There is a hole in the middle of each vertebra, which the spinal cord fits through.

Each year, nearly 7 million people in the US are treated for a broken bone.

The ribs form a protective cage (literally called the ribcage) around vital organs such as the heart and lungs. Most people have 12 pairs of ribs, making 24 altogether, but some people are born with only 11 pairs, and others get an extra rib or two!

TWISTS

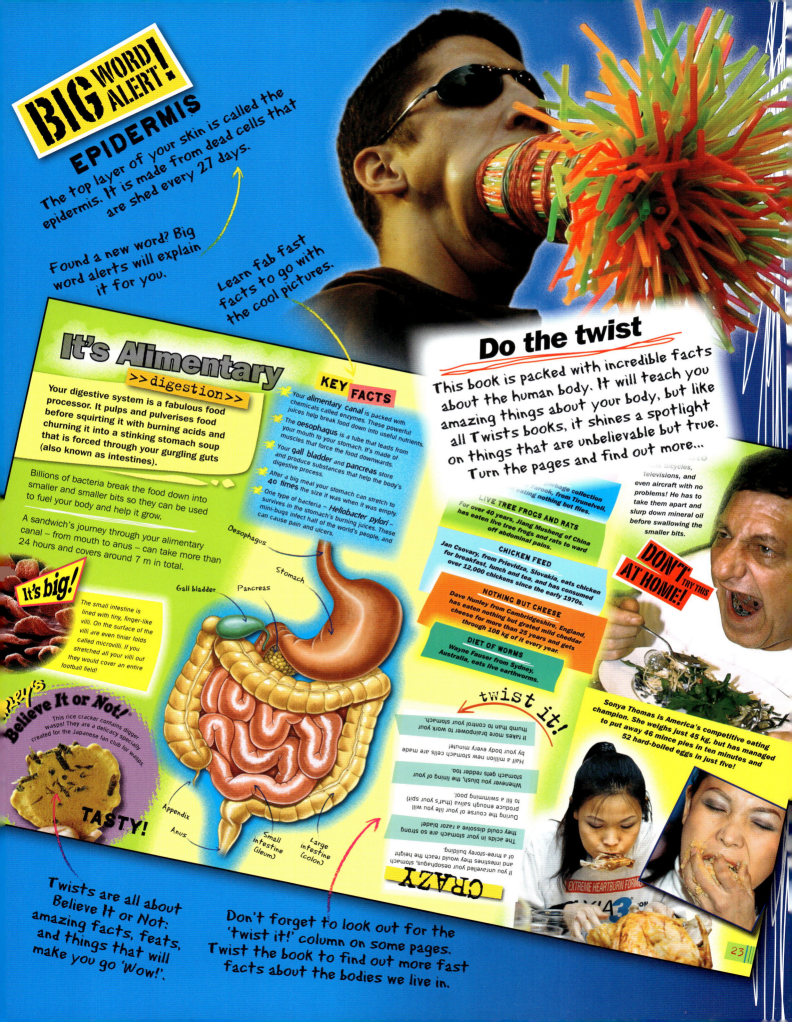

BIG WORD ALERT!

EPIDERMIS

The top layer of your skin is called the epidermis. It is made from dead cells that are shed every 27 days.

Found a new word? Big word alerts will explain it for you.

Learn fab fast facts to go with the cool pictures.

It's Alimentary

>>digestion>>

Your digestive system is a fabulous food processor. It pulps and pulverises food before squirting it with burning acids and churning it into a stinking stomach soup that is forced through your gurgling guts (also known as intestines).

Billions of bacteria break the food down into smaller and smaller bits so they can be used to fuel your body and help it grow.

A sandwich's journey through your alimentary canal – from mouth to anus – can take more than 24 hours and covers around 7 m in total.

KEY FACTS

* Your **alimentary canal** is packed with chemicals called enzymes. These powerful juices help break food down into useful nutrients.
* The **oesophagus** is a tube that leads from your mouth to your stomach. It's made of muscles that force the food downwards.
* Your **gall bladder** and **pancreas** store and produce substances that help the body's digestive process.
* After a big meal your stomach can stretch to **40 times** the size it was when it was empty.
* One type of bacteria – *Helicobacter pylori* – survives in the stomach's burning juices. These mini-bugs infect half of the world's people, and can cause pain and ulcers.

It's big!

The small intestine is lined with tiny, finger-like villi. On the surface of the villi are even tinier folds called microvilli. If you stretched all your villi out they would cover an entire football field!

Believe It or Not!

This rice cracker contains digger wasps! They are a delicacy specially created for the Japanese fan club for wasps.

TASTY!

Oesophagus

Gall bladder

Pancreas

Stomach

Appendix

Anus

Small intestine (ileum)

Large intestine (colon)

Do the twist

This book is packed with incredible facts about the human body. It will teach you amazing things about your body, but like all Twists books, it shines a spotlight on things that are unbelievable but true. Turn the pages and find out more...

...k bicycles, televisions, and even aircraft with no problems! He has to take them apart and slurp down mineral oil before swallowing the smaller bits.

...garbage collection ...Farook, from Tirunelveli, ...eating nothing but flies.

LIVE TREE FROGS AND RATS
For over 40 years, Jiang Musheng of China has eaten live tree frogs and rats to ward off abdominal pains.

CHICKEN FEED
Jan Csovary, from Prievidza, Slovakia, eats chicken for breakfast, lunch and tea, and has consumed over 12,000 chickens since the early 1970s.

NOTHING BUT CHEESE
Dave Nunley from Cambridgeshire, England, has eaten nothing but grated mild cheddar cheese for more than 25 years and gets through 108 kg of it every year.

DIET OF WORMS
Wayne Fauser from Sydney, Australia, eats live earthworms.

DON'T TRY THIS AT HOME!

Sonya Thomas is America's competitive eating champion. She weighs just 45 kg, but has managed to put away 46 mince pies in ten minutes and 52 hard-boiled eggs in just five!

twist it!

It takes more brainpower to work your thumb than to control your stomach.

Half a million new stomach cells are made by your body every minute!

Whenever you blush, the lining of your stomach gets redder too.

During the course of your life you will produce enough saliva (that's your spit) to fill a swimming pool.

The acids in your stomach are so strong they could dissolve a razor blade!

If you unravelled your oesophagus, stomach and intestines they would reach the height of a three-storey building.

CRAZY

Twists are all about Believe It or Not: amazing facts, feats, and things that will make you go 'Wow!'.

Don't forget to look out for the 'twist it!' column on some pages. Twist the book to find out more fast facts about the bodies we live in.

Hold it a Up!

>> bones >>

Let's have a look...

Skull

Ball and socket joint

Humerus

Vertebra

Sternum

Rib

Pelvis

Radius

Ulna

CLEVER!

Some bones contain bone marrow, where blood cells are made.

AMAZING!

Bone tissue can be spongy or hard. Spongy bone is full of holes, which makes it both incredibly strong and lightweight.

Inside your body there's a gigantic jigsaw puzzle holding you up. Made from up to 300 bones, your skeleton stops you from squelching and slopping all over the floor.

Bones are terrifically tough. In fact, a piece of bone the size of a matchbox is four times tougher than concrete! That's why the most precious body bits are protected by bony armour, such as the skull, rib cage and pelvis.

Bones are living, growing parts of your body and make up around 20% of your weight. If you break – or fracture – a bone, your body will instantly get to work on the repair job, growing new spongy bone in less than two weeks!

Femur

Hinge joint

Fibula

Tibia

Bones don't bend, but they can move. Places where they meet are called joints. These joints are held together by tough connecting tissue called ligaments.

Ripley's Believe It or Not!®

There are **206 bones** in an adult's body. Half of them are in the feet (52) and hands (54). Babies have around 300 bones, but some of these join together as the baby grows.

Minerals, such as calcium, make your bones hard. If you sucked all the minerals out of a leg bone, it wouldn't be much stronger than a piece of string.

Your bones are **softer than an adult's.** They won't fully harden until you are 18 years old.

You will probably bend – or flex – your finger joints more than **25 million** times in a lifetime: even more if you play an instrument!

Humans have tail bones. Called the coccyx (say cox-six), this part of your spine helps you lift heavy objects and keep balanced.

Most people have 12 pairs of ribs, making 24 in total. However, one person out of every 500 has 13 or 11 pairs instead!

Twenty years ago amazingly flexible **Ray Gonzales** discovered that he had such flexible joints that he could twist his body 180 degrees so that his feet point completely the wrong way. Great for walking backwards!

DON'T TRY THIS AT HOME!

HOW LOW CAN YOU GO?

Limbo-skating, shown off here by Aniket Chindak from India, involves stretching your ligaments so much that the body can fold almost flat. With enough speed, Aniket can roller skate underneath a parked car!

Use the Force

No matter how much you grow, there are parts of your body that shrink – muscles! Thankfully, these bundles of mighty fibres only get smaller to move a bone, before returning to their normal size.

Xie Tianzhuang, an 87 year old from China, lifted 14 bricks with his teeth in 2005. The bricks weighed 35 kg altogether.

Muscles give you power; they make up half your body weight and provide the pulling forces that allow you to bend an arm or lift a foot. Without your muscles – whether they're feeble or fearsome – you simply wouldn't be able to move. You've got 100 just in your head, face and neck!

MOVE IT!

Muscles usually work in pairs. Bend your arm and flex your biceps to see the muscle bulge as it shortens. As you relax your arm the biceps relaxes and the triceps muscle below contracts (becomes shorter).

There are three types of muscle. **Skeletal muscle** helps you move and **smooth muscle** does jobs such as keeping food travelling through your digestive system. **Cardiac muscle** makes your heart pump blood. Skeletal muscles are attached to bones by tough fibres, called tendons.

Bent arm – biceps is contracted.

The triceps muscle will contract to straighten the arm again.

PUCKER UP!
You use 11 face muscles to frown, 12 to smile and 20 to kiss!

Keep on truckin'

The Rev. Jon Bruney, from Indiana, USA, is famous for his strongman achievements, such as bending steel bars and tearing phone directories in half. In 2004 he and two other strongmen joined forces to pull a 15-tonne trailer for 1.5 km.

BIG WORD ALERT!

GLUTEUS MAXIMUS
The biggest muscle in your body is called the gluteus maximus. It's in your bottom.

twist it!

Way back in the 1920s performer Clarence Willard of the USA amazed audiences by growing 15 cm in height, just by stretching the muscles of his knees, hips and throat.

The tiniest muscle in the body is called the stirrup. You have one inside each ear, and it is no bigger than this number 1.

Your body is about two-thirds water, and about half of this is contained in your muscles.

Humans have more than 600 muscles in their bodies, but caterpillars have more than 4,000!

Turn your foot outwards and you will be using 13 different muscles in your leg and 20 in the foot. Taking a simple step forwards uses 54 muscles!

MEGA MUSCLES

need a lift?

Need a lift? Ask John Evans – he could possibly carry you and your car on his head! His best effort is balancing a car weighing 160 kg for 33 seconds.

9

Under Pressure

>> blood >>

Blood: you know it as the oozy red stuff that pours out when you cut yourself. But about 5 litres of this thick liquid is racing around your body, keeping everything in good order. Lose half of your blood and you'll drop dead!

Blood is like a river of life. It carries oxygen and nutrients to every cell, and mops up all the toxic waste. It's also at the front line of your body's defence system. White blood cells track down and kill any nasty bugs that are out to damage, or even destroy, you.

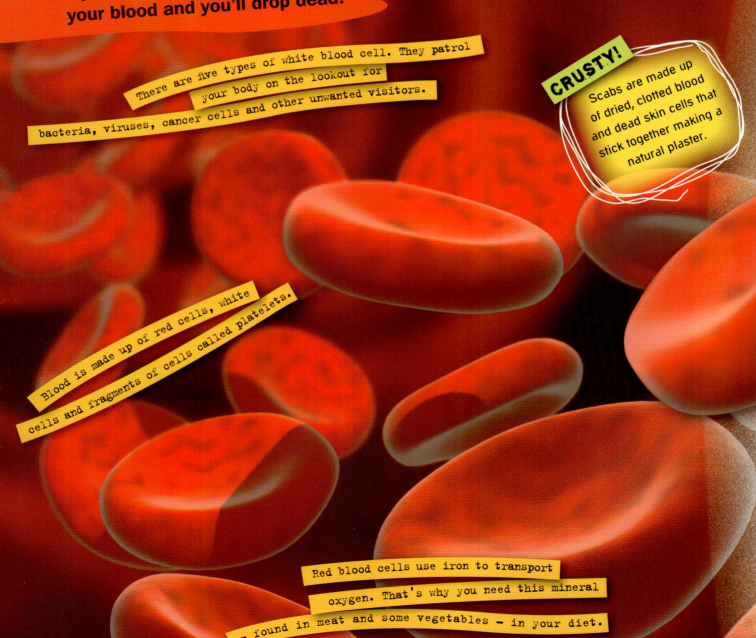

There are five types of white blood cell. They patrol your body on the lookout for bacteria, viruses, cancer cells and other unwanted visitors.

CRUSTY!

Scabs are made up of dried, clotted blood and dead skin cells that stick together making a natural plaster.

Blood is made up of red cells, white cells and fragments of cells called platelets.

Red blood cells use iron to transport oxygen. That's why you need this mineral – found in meat and some vegetables – in your diet.

BIG WORD ALERT!

NUTRIENTS

Substances that provide goodness for growth and health, like fats, proteins, and carbohydrates. One of the roles of blood is to carry nutrients around the body.

Artery wall

Red blood cell

Plasma

Blood cells float in a fluid called plasma. Blood makes up about 8% of your body weight.

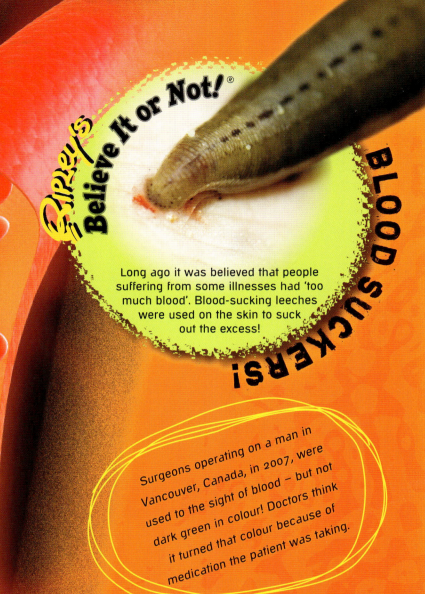

Ripley's Believe It or Not!®

BLOOD SUCKERS!

Long ago it was believed that people suffering from some illnesses had 'too much blood'. Blood-sucking leeches were used on the skin to suck out the excess!

Surgeons operating on a man in Vancouver, Canada, in 2007, were used to the sight of blood – but not dark green in colour! Doctors think it turned that colour because of medication the patient was taking.

blood is brilliant

✳ **Bone marrow** makes around 2 million red blood cells every second.

✳ A single red blood cell can carry about one billion packets of oxygen around your body. You have **25 trillion red blood cells**...so that's a lot of oxygen!

✳ **One drop** of blood contains around 5 million red blood cells.

✳ **Blood** can be taken from one human body and put into another, in a life-saving procedure called a transfusion. Frank Loose of Germany has donated some of his own blood more than 800 times, and has saved dozens of lives with his gift.

Take Heart

In the centre of your chest is your heart. It's a powerful, pumping organ that sends blood whizzing around a network of blood vessels at speeds of 270 km a day!

When your heart beats it pumps blood from inside the heart around your body, through blood vessels. In between beats your heart fills with blood again. Your blood carries oxygen to all parts of your body to make them work.

It gets this oxygen from your lungs when you breathe in. This oxygen-rich blood is taken to your heart to be pumped around the body.

When the blood has delivered the oxygen to your body it comes back to the heart to be pumped out again to collect more oxygen from the lungs.

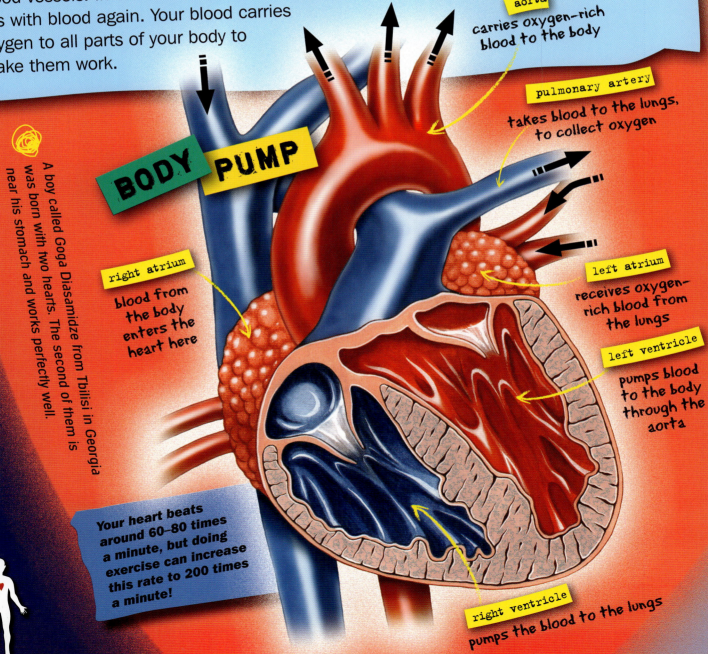

BODY PUMP

aorta
carries oxygen-rich blood to the body

pulmonary artery
takes blood to the lungs, to collect oxygen

right atrium
blood from the body enters the heart here

left atrium
receives oxygen-rich blood from the lungs

left ventricle
pumps blood to the body through the aorta

right ventricle
pumps the blood to the lungs

A boy called Goga Diasamidze from Tbilisi in Georgia was born with two hearts. The second of them is near his stomach and works perfectly well.

Your heart beats around 60–80 times a minute, but doing exercise can increase this rate to 200 times a minute!

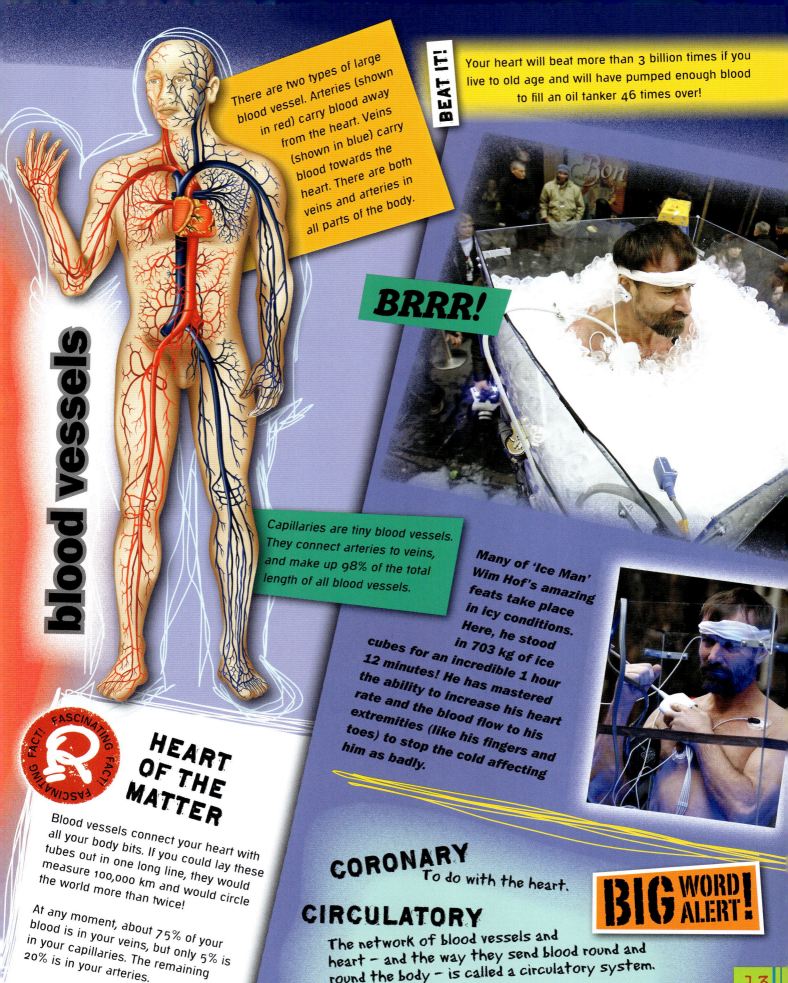

There are two types of large blood vessel. Arteries (shown in red) carry blood away from the heart. Veins (shown in blue) carry blood towards the heart. There are both veins and arteries in all parts of the body.

blood vessels

BEAT IT!

Your heart will beat more than 3 billion times if you live to old age and will have pumped enough blood to fill an oil tanker 46 times over!

BRRR!

Capillaries are tiny blood vessels. They connect arteries to veins, and make up 98% of the total length of all blood vessels.

Many of 'Ice Man' Wim Hof's amazing feats take place in icy conditions. Here, he stood in 703 kg of ice cubes for an incredible 1 hour 12 minutes! He has mastered the ability to increase his heart rate and the blood flow to his extremities (like his fingers and toes) to stop the cold affecting him as badly.

HEART OF THE MATTER

FASCINATING FACT!

Blood vessels connect your heart with all your body bits. If you could lay these tubes out in one long line, they would measure 100,000 km and would circle the world more than twice!

At any moment, about 75% of your blood is in your veins, but only 5% is in your capillaries. The remaining 20% is in your arteries.

CORONARY
To do with the heart.

CIRCULATORY
The network of blood vessels and heart – and the way they send blood round and round the body – is called a circulatory system.

BIG WORD ALERT!

13

Seeing is Believing

>> eyes >>

Eyes are jelly-filled cameras and your body's number-one sense organs. All day long your eyes keep your brain busy, passing it masses of information about the world around you.

Rays of light pour into your eyes, where clear lenses focus them to make a crisp, clean image. Nerves zap info about the image to the brain, which has the tricky task of turning those nerve signals into vision. It can even combine the images from both eyes to make a single 3-D picture.

It takes six muscles to move each eyeball, so you can get a good view all around. If you spy something sad, your tears drain into tiny holes in the corner of your eyes, and flow into your nose. That's why your nose runs when you cry!

Lens

Aqueous humour

Ligaments

Pupil

Iris

Cornea

EYE SPY
Human eye muscles move around 10,000 times a day!

Student Jalisa Mae Thompson can pop her eyeballs so far out of their sockets they hardly look real!

14

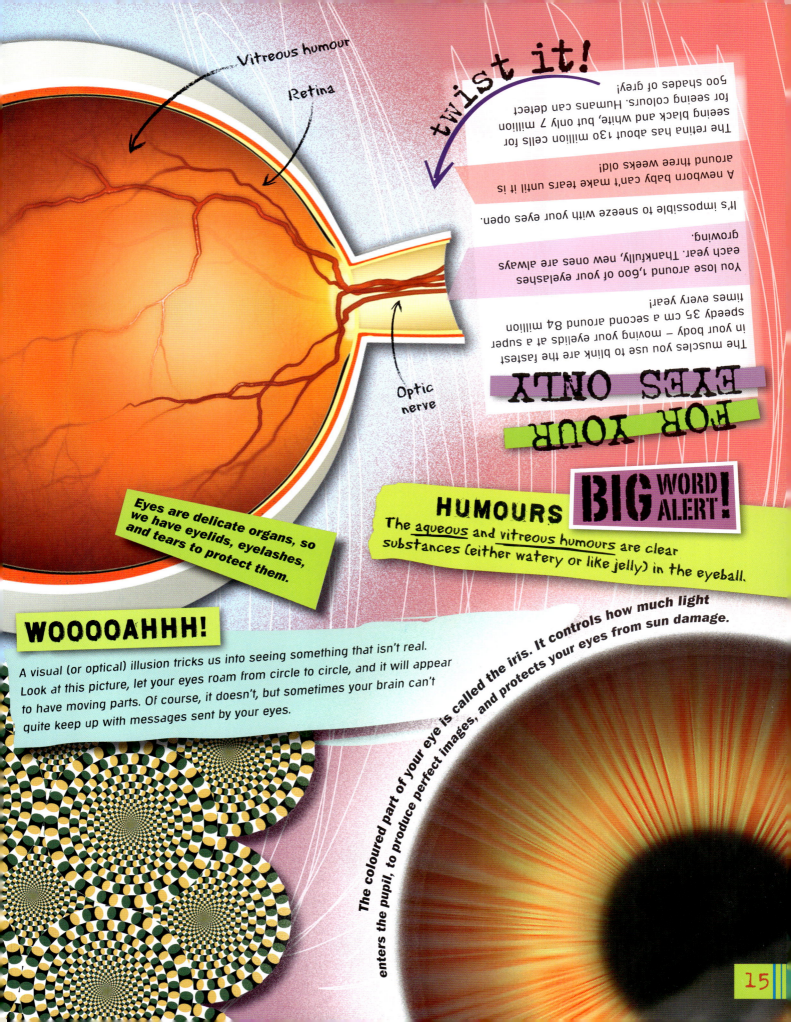

Vitreous humour

Retina

Optic nerve

twist it!

The retina has about 130 million cells for seeing black and white, but only 7 million for seeing colours. Humans can detect 500 shades of grey!

A newborn baby can't make tears until it is around three weeks old!

It's impossible to sneeze with your eyes open.

You lose around 1,600 of your eyelashes each year. Thankfully, new ones are always growing.

The muscles you use to blink are the fastest in your body – moving your eyelids at a super speedy 35 cm a second around 84 million times every year!

FOR YOUR EYES ONLY

BIG WORD ALERT!

HUMOURS
The <u>aqueous</u> and vitreous humours are clear substances (either watery or like jelly) in the eyeball.

Eyes are delicate organs, so we have eyelids, eyelashes, and tears to protect them.

WOOOOAHHH!

A visual (or optical) illusion tricks us into seeing something that isn't real. Look at this picture, let your eyes roam from circle to circle, and it will appear to have moving parts. Of course, it doesn't, but sometimes your brain can't quite keep up with messages sent by your eyes.

The coloured part of your eye is called the iris. It controls how much light enters the pupil, to produce perfect images, and protects your eyes from sun damage.

15

Surround Sound

>> ears >>

GET THE BALANCE RIGHT

Listen carefully – it's time to find out how ears hear. These auditory organs don't just help you to sense sound: they stop you from falling over, every time you take a step!

Squashed next to the cochlea is an organ of balance. It is made up of three tubes, all filled with liquid. If you spin round, that liquid swishes about, making you dizzy!

That fleshy flap stuck to the side of your head is just one part of an ear. Each flap, or pinna, sends sound down your ear canal to the eardrum, which vibrates. Those vibrations shimmy through the tiny hammer, anvil and stirrup bones into a shell-shaped organ, called the cochlea.

The cochlea is where the real business of hearing happens. Sound is turned into nerve impulses and sent at lightning speed to the brain. And hey presto – you can hear!

Your smallest bones – stirrups – are in your ears. They measure 2.6 mm long and weigh 0.004 g.

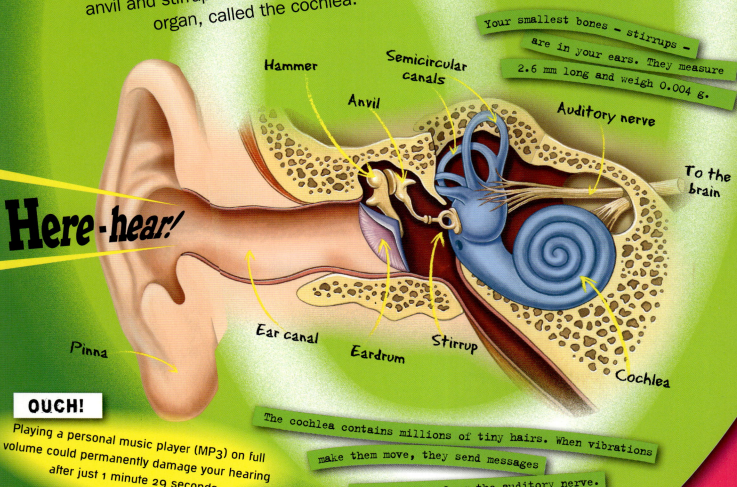

Here - hear!

Hammer

Semicircular canals

Anvil

Auditory nerve

To the brain

Pinna

Ear canal

Eardrum

Stirrup

Cochlea

OUCH!

Playing a personal music player (MP3) on full volume could permanently damage your hearing after just 1 minute 29 seconds.

The cochlea contains millions of tiny hairs. When vibrations make them move, they send messages to the brain along the auditory nerve.

Beethoven was a famous composer of classical music. He continued to write and perform great music even when he lost his hearing!

Wei Mingtang from China has leaky ears. He attaches a hose to them, and then blows out candles or inflates balloons!

Earwax and ear hair protect your ears, and even prevent insects from nesting in the ear canal!

Earwax can be yellow, orange or brown and gross old bits drop out of your ears all the time.

People used to believe that earwigs would climb into ears while people slept, and burrow into their brains to lay their eggs. It's not true, honestly!

twist it!

STEADY AS YOU GO

Balancing on a high wire is tricky enough, but this guy managed to pedal his bike 30 m above the ground without falling off!

BIG WORD ALERT!

AUDITORY
To do with hearing.

It may sound strange (ha ha!) but many people around the world enjoy performing feats of 'ear strength'. This man, celebrating Chinese New Year in Beijing, is just one of several choosing to pull vehicles along with his ear. Ouch!

Hey, you've got something in your ear! Narayan Rasad Pal of India proudly shows off the long strands of hair that grow from his ears. They measure an incredible 10 cm!

千斤人绝活

Staggering Senses

>> taste, touch and more! >>

Close your eyes and touch the tip of your nose with a finger. Easy isn't it? But how did you know where your nose is? Thanks to your staggering senses you've got up-to-date nuggets of info whizzing to your brain all of the time.

How many senses do you have? People used to say we have five: we can see, hear, touch, smell and taste. But now we know there are loads more. Feelings such as cold and hunger are all part of your body's sensory world.

RUMBLE!

Got tummy rumbles and pain in your belly? Your body is telling you to eat – now! You could make like Japan's Takeru Kobayashi, international champion hot-dog eater. In 2005 he retained his title by eating 49 hot dogs in 12 minutes. His personal best is an unbelievable 53.5 hot dogs in that time!

BRRR!

Getting so cold it hurts? Time to put on your winter woollies or go somewhere warm, before you freeze to death. Ice swimmer Lewis Pugh swam 1 km in the Antarctic wearing only a swimming cap, goggles and trunks, in a temperature of 0°C. He was in the water for 18 minutes 10 seconds and described the feeling as a 'screaming pain all over his body'.

FASCINATING FACT

The makers of Stilton cheese have launched their own perfume with the same smell!

Your brain collects sensory information from the rest of your body – and tells you how to react to it all.

FASCINATING FACT

It takes just 0.02 of a second for your brain to realise when you've dropped a book on your toe.

YUM!

Taste is an important sense – it can warn you that something isn't good for you to put in your mouth.

FASCINATING FACT

An ice-cream parlour in Nice, France, offers its customers up to 70 different flavours of ice cream, including tomato and basil, black olive, and chewing gum!

OUCH!

Some pains keep you from harm or tell you it's time to visit the doctor. Not so for Miss Electra, who had 2 million volts of electricity passed through her body and out of her fingertips for a TV show in Hollywood. She doesn't feel any pain when this takes place!

KEY FACTS

* Your senses are there to tell your brain what is going on inside, and outside, the body.

* Your brain then knows if things are changing, and can decide when to make your body react – perhaps to keep you safe, or get some food or drink, for example.

* The information is sent to your brain along nerves.

SNIFF!

Pongs and stenches tell us to stay away – whiffy food might be covered in nasty bacteria. Mind you, blue cheese such as Stilton smells strong but is safe to eat. The blue veins are mould caused by bacteria, and if you think they smell like stinky feet, you'd be right – it can be the same bacteria.

OOPS!

Stumbling, tripping and falling over – it happens to us all, but most of the time your body is great at keeping your limbs in the right place, and balanced. Shame it only goes wrong when everyone is looking!

Open Up!

Your mouth is home to 10,000 taste buds, up to 32 teeth and billions of bacteria. In fact, there are more bacteria in your mouth than there are people on the planet!

A mouth is a dark hole with lots of jobs to do, from chewing and crunching to coughing, swallowing, tasting and talking. Food begins its digestive journey in your mouth, where teeth grind it into little pieces and morsels get juiced up with sloppy saliva. Thanks to the taste buds on your tongue you can sense flavours – such as salty, sour, sweet and bitter – and either enjoy your snack-attack, or choose to spit out yukky bits.

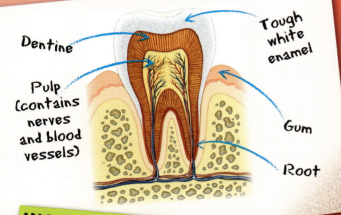

Dentine

Tough white enamel

Pulp (contains nerves and blood vessels)

Gum

Root

INSIDE A TOOTH

BABY TEETH
Your teeth started growing about six months before you were born!

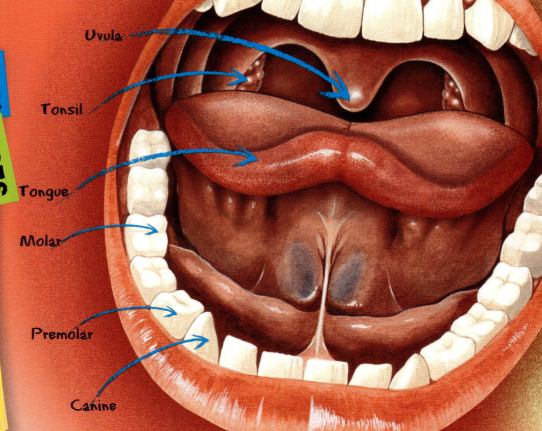

Lips

Incisor

Gum

Uvula

Tonsil

Tongue

Molar

Premolar

Canine

KEY FACTS

There are more than **500 types of bacteria** in your mouth. Most of them are helpful bugs, but the bad ones can rot your teeth or give you stinky breath.

You use your jaws, lips and tongue to speak. Babies' first sounds include 'coo', 'ba ba' and 'da da'.

Girls are usually better at identifying flavours than boys, but boys prefer stronger flavours than girls. Teenagers don't like sour-tasting food!

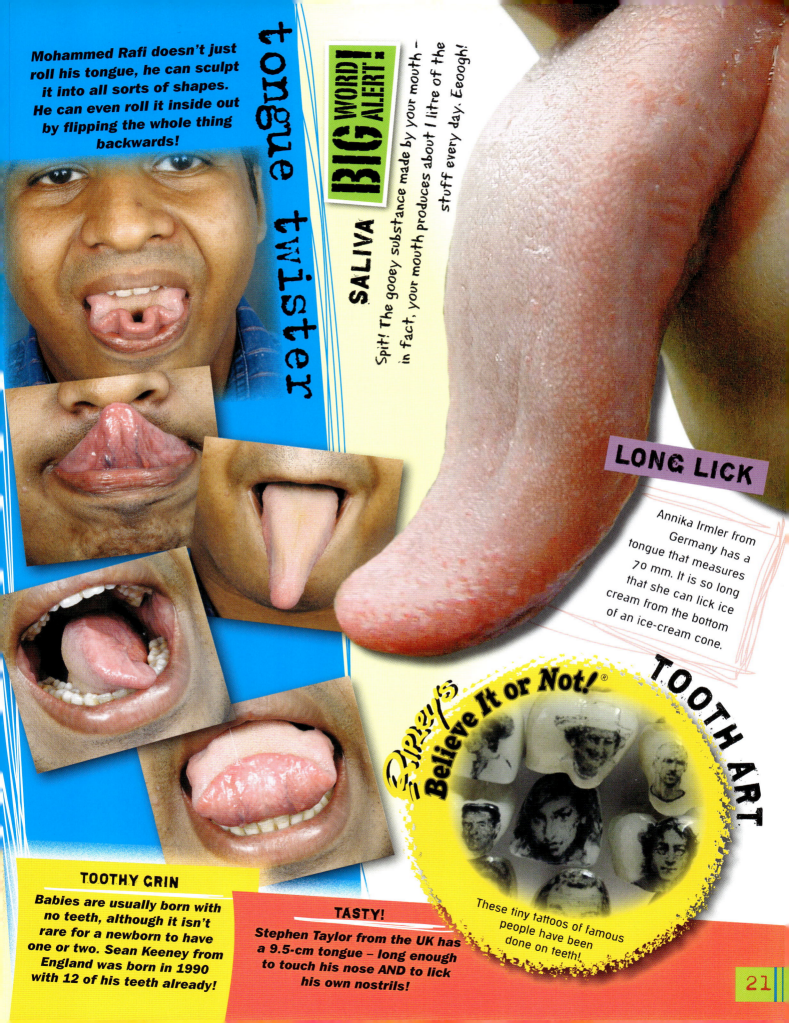

tongue twister

Mohammed Rafi doesn't just roll his tongue, he can sculpt it into all sorts of shapes. He can even roll it inside out by flipping the whole thing backwards!

BIG WORD ALERT!

SALIVA

Spit! The gooey substance made by your mouth – in fact, your mouth produces about 1 litre of the stuff every day. Eeoogh!

LONG LICK

Annika Irmler from Germany has a tongue that measures 70 mm. It is so long that she can lick ice cream from the bottom of an ice-cream cone.

TOOTH ART

Ripley's Believe It or Not!®

These tiny tattoos of famous people have been done on teeth!

TOOTHY GRIN

Babies are usually born with no teeth, although it isn't rare for a newborn to have one or two. Sean Keeney from England was born in 1990 with 12 of his teeth already!

TASTY!

Stephen Taylor from the UK has a 9.5-cm tongue – long enough to touch his nose AND to lick his own nostrils!

It's Alimentary

>> digestion >>

Your digestive system is a fabulous food processor. It pulps and pulverises food before squirting it with burning acids and churning it into a stinking stomach soup that is forced through your gurgling guts (also known as intestines).

Billions of bacteria break the food down into smaller and smaller bits so they can be used to fuel your body and help it grow.

A sandwich's journey through your alimentary canal – from mouth to anus – can take more than 24 hours and covers around 7 m in total.

It's big!

The small intestine is lined with tiny, finger-like villi. On the surface of the villi are even tinier folds called microvilli. If you stretched all your villi out they would cover an entire football field!

Ripley's Believe It or Not!®

This rice cracker contains digger wasps! They are a delicacy specially created for the Japanese fan club for wasps.

TASTY!

* Your **alimentary canal** is packed with chemicals called enzymes. These powerful juices help break food down into useful nutrients.

* The **oesophagus** is a tube that leads from your mouth to your stomach. It's made of muscles that force the food downwards.

* Your **gall bladder** and **pancreas** store and produce substances that help the body's digestive process.

* After a big meal your stomach can stretch to **40 times** the size it was when it was empty.

* One type of bacteria – *Heliobacter pylori* – survives in the stomach's burning juices. These mini-bugs infect half of the world's people, and can cause pain and ulcers.

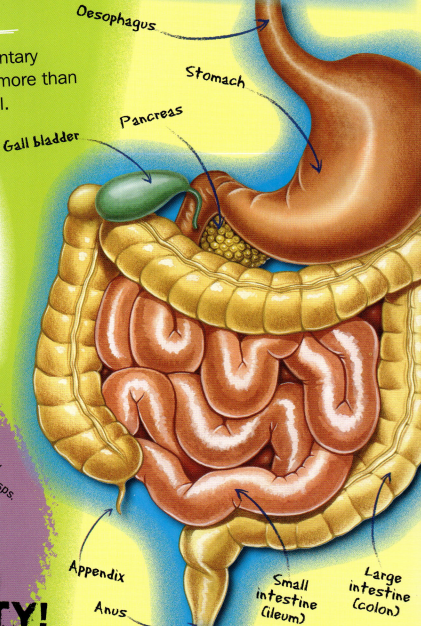

Oesophagus

Stomach

Pancreas

Gall bladder

Appendix

Anus

Small intestine (ileum)

Large intestine (colon)

LIVE SCORPIONS

Father-of-two Hasip Kaya of Turkey has been addicted to eating live scorpions since he was a boy.

FLY FEAST

In protest at his town's garbage collection service, a man named Farook, from Tirunelveli, India, started eating nothing but flies.

LIVE TREE FROGS AND RATS

For over 40 years, Jiang Musheng of China has eaten live tree frogs and rats to ward off abdominal pains.

CHICKEN FEED

Jan Csovary, from Prievidza, Slovakia, eats chicken for breakfast, lunch and tea, and has consumed over 12,000 chickens since the early 1970s.

NOTHING BUT CHEESE

Dave Nunley from Cambridgeshire, England, has eaten nothing but grated mild cheddar cheese for more than 25 years and gets through 108 kg of it every year.

DIET OF WORMS

Wayne Fauser from Sydney, Australia, eats live earthworms.

Michel Lotito eats bicycles, televisions, and even aircraft with no problems! He has to take them apart and slurp down mineral oil before swallowing the smaller bits.

DON'T TRY THIS AT HOME!

Sonya Thomas is America's competitive eating champion. She weighs just 45 kg, but has managed to put away 46 mince pies in ten minutes and 52 hard-boiled eggs in just five!

twist it!

It takes more brainpower to work your thumb than to control your stomach.

Half a million new stomach cells are made by your body every minute!

Whenever you blush, the lining of your stomach gets redder too.

During the course of your life you will produce enough saliva (that's your spit) to fill a swimming pool.

The acids in your stomach are so strong they could dissolve a razor blade!

If you unravelled your oesophagus, stomach and intestines they would reach the height of a three-storey building.

CRAZY

what a Waste

As your food makes its way through your digestive system, your body makes sure that nothing it needs goes to waste. A team of friendly organs slogs away, like a recycling plant, to suck out every last bit of goodness.

Blood vessels carry the nutrients from your food to the liver, where they are sorted, processed, recycled or stored. The rubbish bits are sent packing back to your guts where they join the leftovers to make the solid stuff that leaves your body. It's called faeces (say fee-sees).

Faeces is made up of old blood cells, bits of undigested food, bacteria and water. The liquid waste is called urine and it's actually 96% water.

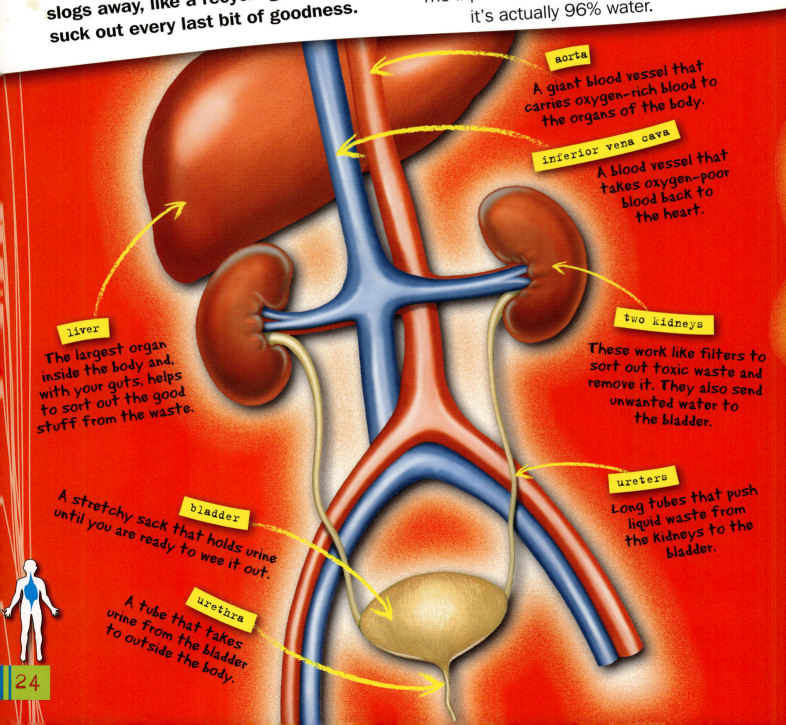

aorta
A giant blood vessel that carries oxygen-rich blood to the organs of the body.

inferior vena cava
A blood vessel that takes oxygen-poor blood back to the heart.

liver
The largest organ inside the body and, with your guts, helps to sort out the good stuff from the waste.

two kidneys
These work like filters to sort out toxic waste and remove it. They also send unwanted water to the bladder.

bladder
A stretchy sack that holds urine until you are ready to wee it out.

ureters
Long tubes that push liquid waste from the kidneys to the bladder.

urethra
A tube that takes urine from the bladder to outside the body.

24

twist it!

FUNNY TUMMY

Sloppy poo is called diarrhoea (say die-ar-ee-ah). It's often caused by nasty bugs – so wash your hands before eating and after using the loo!

Your liver is the second largest organ of your body and it can continue to work if 80% of it is removed. It will even grow back to its previous size!

One person produces enough urine to fill about 270 bathtubs during a lifetime.

Many ancient people believed that drinking their own urine would cure tummy troubles or other digestive disorders. Romans used it in their toothpaste.

Even waste is recycled. Faeces and urine travel from toilets through sewage pipes to sewage plants, where waste matter can be turned into fabulous fertilizer to be spread on farmers' fields.

WASTE PRODUCTS

There are more than one million tiny tubes, or filters, in the kidneys. They are called nephrons and measure around 65 km in total length!

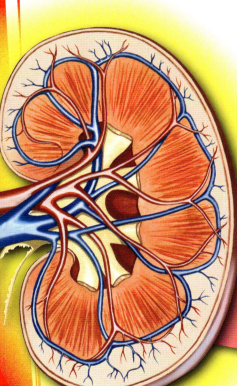

TIME FOR TEA

A restaurant in Kaohsiung, China, is totally toilet themed – diners sit on toilets, eat at basin-style tables, and have their food served in bowls shaped like toilets or waste pots.

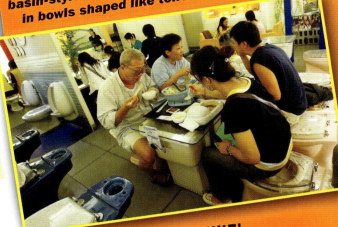

CLEAN MACHINE!

This wacky flying machine was part of a 2003 flying demonstration in France. Don't flush while you're up there!

FEELING FLUSHED!

Fancy finding a snake in your toilet! A 3-m-long boa constrictor appeared in a loo in Manchester, England, and then again in a neighbour's toilet bowl after moving through the sewage system of a block of apartments.

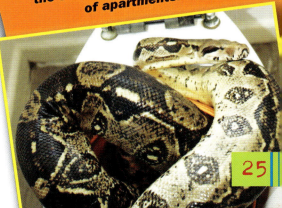

KEY FACTS

The liver has more than 500 different jobs, including cleaning blood, storing vitamins and preparing nutrients to be used by the body.

If you don't drink enough water your kidneys stop water going into your bladder. That makes your wee look darker.

Minerals in urine can turn into solid stones, called bladder stones, which have to be removed by a doctor.

Life's a Gas

>> breathing >>

Lungs are lazy life-savers. With no muscles of their own, these air-filled puffers rely on rib muscles and a diaphragm to work. Every breath you take draws air into your lungs, which are each packed with 300 million alveoli. These thin-skinned sacs are swap shops, where oxygen is traded for carbon dioxide, the waste gas you breathe out.

Oxygen: you can't see it, smell it, touch it or taste it – but without this gas your body would pack up in minutes. Thanks to your lungs you can concentrate on other stuff while you breathe in oxygen – more than 10 million times every year!

Phew!

With six billion people breathing in oxygen you may expect we'd run out one day. Fortunately, when green plants respire they use up carbon dioxide, and produce oxygen. Phew!

Air-mazing

Air contains 21% oxygen. Breathing pure oxygen is actually dangerous.

look inside your lungs!

BREATHE OUT

BREATHE IN

Trachea

Bronchi

Bronchus

Bronchioles

At the top of the trachea is a voice box, or larynx. Passing air through the larynx as you breathe out makes your vocal cords vibrate, creating sound. Breathing in and talking at the same time is almost impossible – try it!

Left lung

Right lung

RESPIRATION

Breathing in and out. All the body bits that get oxygen from the air, and pass it into the blood stream, are called the respiratory system.

LUNGS—
LET'S LOOK CLOSER

Bronchiole

Artery from heart

Deoxygenated blood from heart

Oxygenated blood to heart

Alveoli

BIG WORD ALERT!

DEEP BREATH

twist it!

You breathe around 20 times a minute – that's 700 million times during an average lifetime.

Every day you breathe in enough air to fill 1,000 party balloons. (But we don't recommend it!)

Your lungs contain around 300,000 capillaries (tiny blood vessels). If they were stretched out they would measure 2,400 km!

The loudest scream ever measured was 129 decibels – that's loud enough to make your ears hurt.

In June 2008, freediver Herbert Nitsch from Austria used just the air in his lungs to sink to a record-breaking 214 m in the ocean. During the dive, which took 4 minutes 24 seconds, his lungs shrank to the size of a fist and filled with blood, returning to normal at the surface.

David Merlini spent 10 minutes 17 seconds chained and handcuffed underwater in 2007, without air. He escaped from the five sets of handcuffs and 27 kg of chains all without taking a single breath.

Under Command

Electrical messages buzz around your body at speeds of 100 m/second – that's ten times faster than the fastest human has ever run, and about one-third of the speed of sound.

Toddlers and teenagers have far more neurons (nerve cells) than adults or kids of other ages.

These speedy signals whizz backwards and forwards on the body's super-highways – your nerves – and are controlled by the brain. You've got a lot of nerve: if all of your body's nerves were spread end to end they would measure more than 150,000 km!

Nerves instruct muscles to move, and send back messages to the brain about what's happening to your body. Like a bossy headteacher, they have everything under their command.

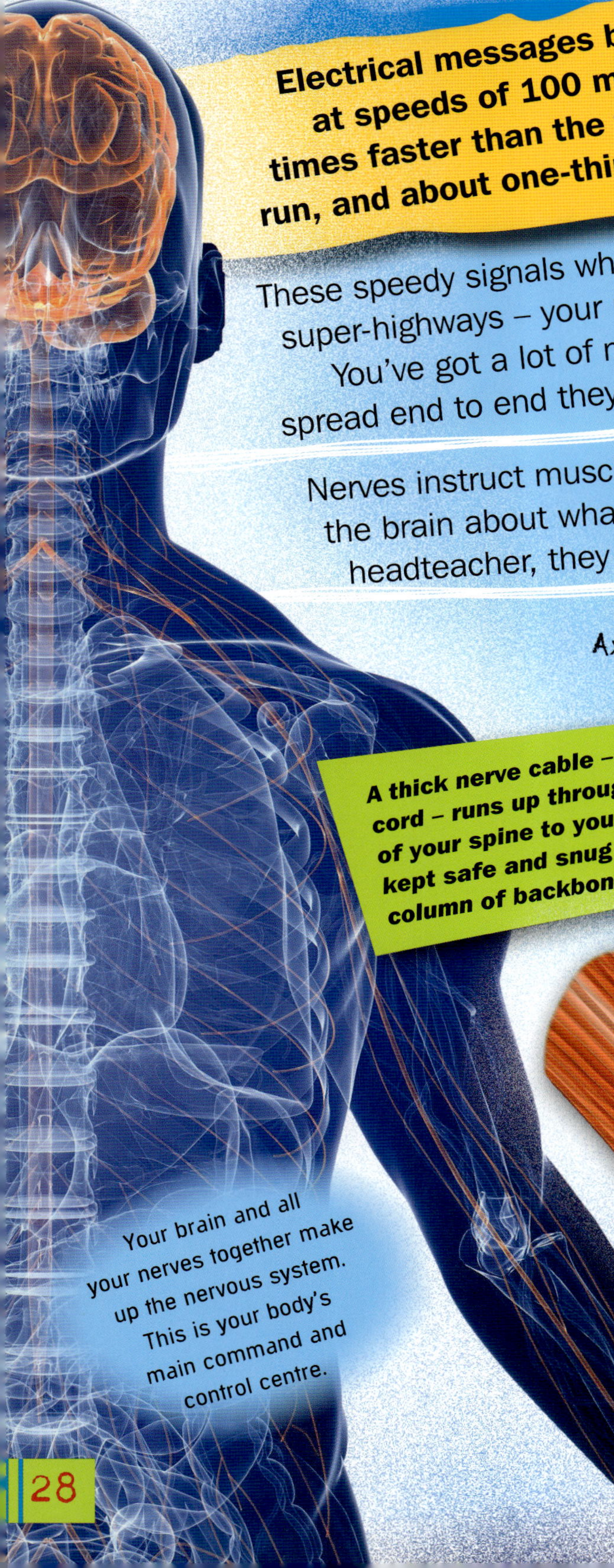

Axon

nervous twitch?

A thick nerve cable – the spinal cord – runs up through the centre of your spine to your brain. It's kept safe and snug inside a column of backbones.

Muscle fibre

Junction between nerve cell and muscle

Nerve cell

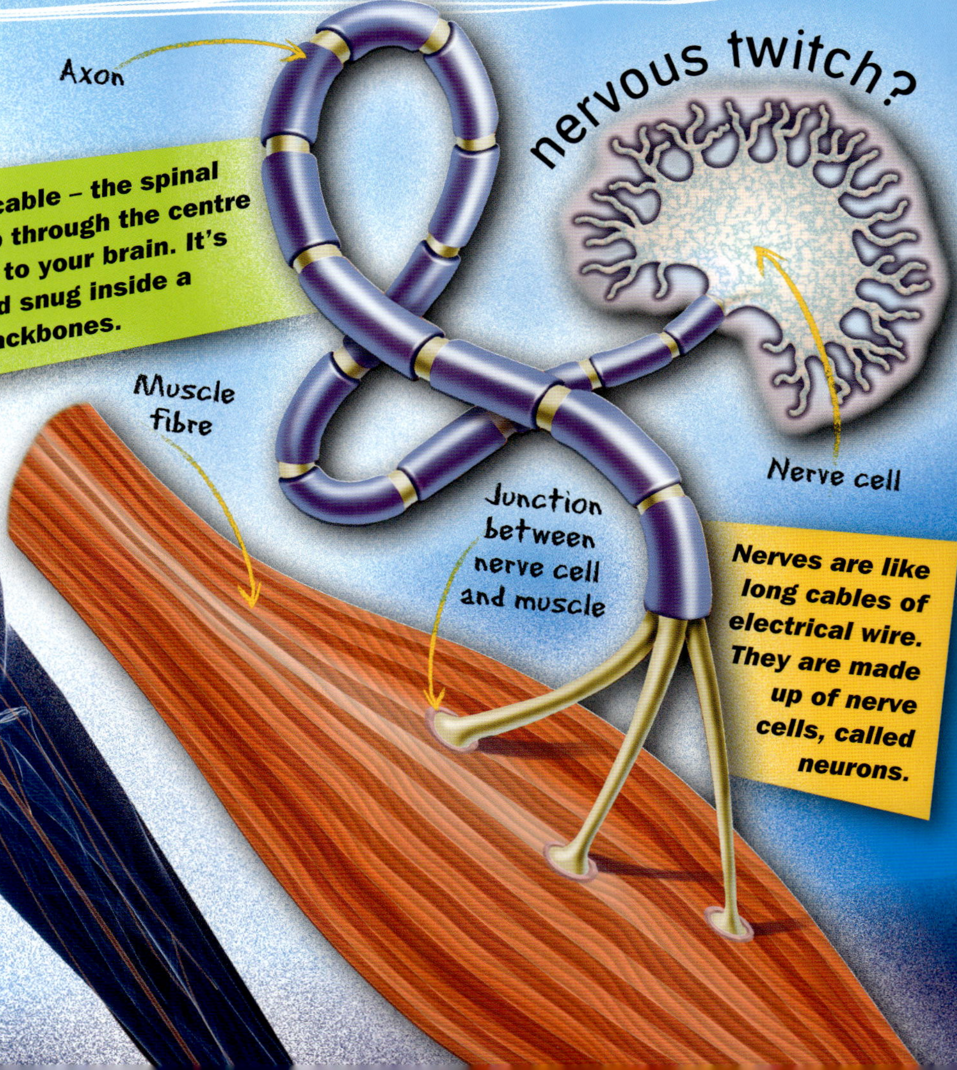

Nerves are like long cables of electrical wire. They are made up of nerve cells, called neurons.

Your brain and all your nerves together make up the nervous system. This is your body's main command and control centre.

LOOK OUT!

Catch! Entertainer Nathan Zorchak lives on his nerves, juggling with three chainsaws whizzing past his nose!

STEADY!

You want quick reactions? Look no further than Australian Anthony Kelly, who can catch flying arrows and – wearing a blindfold – speeding paintballs!

SNAKE KISSER

In Malaysia in 2006, Shahimi Abdul Hamid kissed a wild, venomous king cobra 51 times in three minutes, using his quick reflexes to dodge bites from the 5-m snake.

NOT FUNNY

The nerves in your elbow run close to the skin, which is why a knock to your 'funny bone' feels so weird.

ON YOUR NERVES

If you burn your hand, your nerves swing into action, instructing your muscles to move it to safety in just 0.01 seconds.

The longest cells in your body are found in your brain. Stretched out, each one would measure up to 10 m long.

Professor Kevin Warwick studies robot technology. He has had silicon chips inserted into his body, which connect his nervous system to a computer. Now he can control doors and lights without lifting a finger!

twist it!

Uncover your Cover

>> skin >>

No thicker than 20 pages of this book, yet making up 16% of your weight, your skin works hard for your body!

Here are just some of its jobs: it stops your body soaking up water like a sponge, prevents your blood from boiling or freezing, keeps bugs and bacteria out of your insides, and even senses pain and touch. But that's not all: 50 million bacteria call your skin home!

Skin is the body's largest organ and a piece no larger than a postage stamp holds 650 sweat glands, 20 blood vessels and 1,000 nerve endings.

DON'T BE BLUE!

Except Paul Karason can't help it. His skin has turned blue after treating a skin complaint with an ointment containing silver. He has also been drinking 'colloidal silver' for about 15 years, which may have helped with his colour change. It might even have turned his insides blue, too!

GROSS!

A million dust mites live in your mattress and pillow. They feed on the dead skin cells that fall off your body at night.

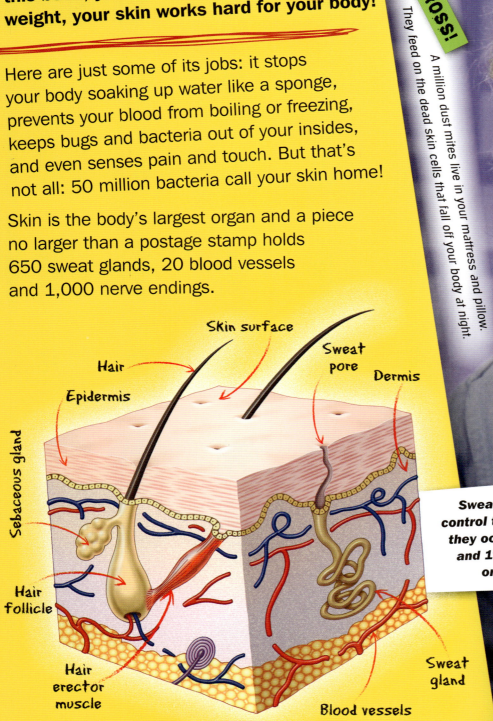

- Skin surface
- Hair
- Epidermis
- Sweat pore
- Dermis
- Sebaceous gland
- Hair follicle
- Hair erector muscle
- Blood vessels
- Sweat gland

Sweat glands in your skin help to control temperature. When you are hot they ooze sweat, which is 99% water and 1% salt. As sweat evaporates, or dries, it cools your skin.

Meet the Leopard Man of Skye! The skin of Tom Leppard from Scotland has been tattooed with the markings of the big cat; over 99% of his skin is tattooed, with only the insides of his ears and the bits between his toes having no artwork.

BIG WORD ALERT!

EPIDERMIS

The top layer of your skin is called the epidermis. It is made from dead cells that are shed every 27 days.

Stretch it!

Gary Stretch has a rare skin condition that allows him to stretch it – and stretch it – and stretch it some more. His skin cells are affected so they don't hold together as tightly as they should, and his skin appears very loose on parts of his body.

Twist it!

Lady Gray Rosemary Jacobs of the USA has grey skin. She thinks the change of colour happened after she used nose drops, which contained tiny amounts of the metal silver.

A computer mouse has been invented that can sense people's emotions. By measuring changes in the user's skin, such as sweat and temperature, the mouse can tell if he or she is feeling sad, angry or tired.

If you could peel off an adult's skin and stretch it out on the floor it would measure around 1.5 to 2 sq m and weigh as much as 4 kg.

Feet sweat because there are 250,000 pores (tiny holes) in the soles. Each squirts about 12 teaspoons of sweat a day.

SKINNY FACTS

Hair-raising Tales

Hair today, gone tomorrow! Most of your body is covered in strands of hair, which grow at a snail's pace of just 8 mm a month. After a few years, each strand of hair falls out.

Thankfully, new hairs grow from special cells in your skin, called follicles, all the time. Each follicle can make about 20 new hairs in a lifetime. Hair grows fastest in the summer, but those dozy follicles like to slow down during the night and catch some ZZZZ. Both hair and nails are made from dead cells that are toughened with a protein called keratin, which is surprisingly stretchy.

Testing 1-2-3
Scientists can use one strand of hair to find out a person's age, sex and race.

BIG HAIR!
Aaron Studham sports a magnificent Mohawk hairstyle that reaches 53 cm in height. It takes him an hour – and lots of hairspray – to get the look.

ITCHY
Tran van Hay from Vietnam has not cut his hair for 38 years and it now measures a staggering 6.2 m. He wears it coiled around his head, which keeps the hair neat and tidy, and his head warm.

32

KEY FACTS

- You could live without hair or nails, but they are useful. Hair helps to keep you warm, and nails protect your delicate fingertips from damage – and are dead handy when you have an itch!

- You have hair all over your body except on the palms of your hands, the soles of your feet and your lips. Humans have as many hairs as chimpanzees!

- Blonde, brunette, raven-haired or redhead? You get your hair colour thanks to the skin pigment, melanin.

snip-its and cuttings

- Human hair was used to make soy sauce in some Chinese barber shops, until the government banned it!

- Your toenails contain traces of gold!

- Mats made from human hair were used in San Francisco to mop up oil that had leaked into the San Francisco Bay.

- Blonde people have about 130,000 hairs on their heads. People with red, black or brown hair have up to 40,000 fewer.

HAIR FACE

Larry Gomez was born with a very rare medical condition, which causes thick, dark hair to grow all over his face and body.

SCRATCHY!

Lee Redmond has been growing her fingernails since 1979. She said it was tough trying to open doors or get dressed, but was very proud when her talons reached 84 cm! Sadly, Lee was involved in a car crash in 2009 and her nails all broke off.

Speedy
Fingernails grow about four times faster than toenails.

33

Grow Up!

>> from birth onwards >>

In about 270 days, or 38 weeks, a single cell can grow into a perfect human baby!

At birth the baby weighs around 3.4 kg and measures a mere 50 cm from head to toe – but will increase in weight a massive ten times by the age of ten. From ten to 20 this blooming baby will double in weight and should reach around 1.7 m tall.

ALL CHANGE

The time of growth, when kids develop into adults, is called puberty.

TINY TOT

Babies are supposed to develop inside their mother's womb for 37 to 40 weeks, but tiny Amillia Sonja Taylor was born after only 21 weeks and 6 days. She was only 24 cm long.

Heave!

Two-year-old Salvador Quini, from Argentina, could lift weights heavier than himself – not so much a strongman as a strongboy!

SUPER BABY!

Mexican newborn Antonio Cruz weighed a massive 6.4 kg when he was born – about twice the weight of many new babies. Look how big he is compared to the average-sized baby lying next to him!

MARVELOUS MIRACLE!

day 1 — Size of a fullstop

6 weeks — Size of a lentil

10 weeks — Size of a strawberry

16 weeks — Size of a pear

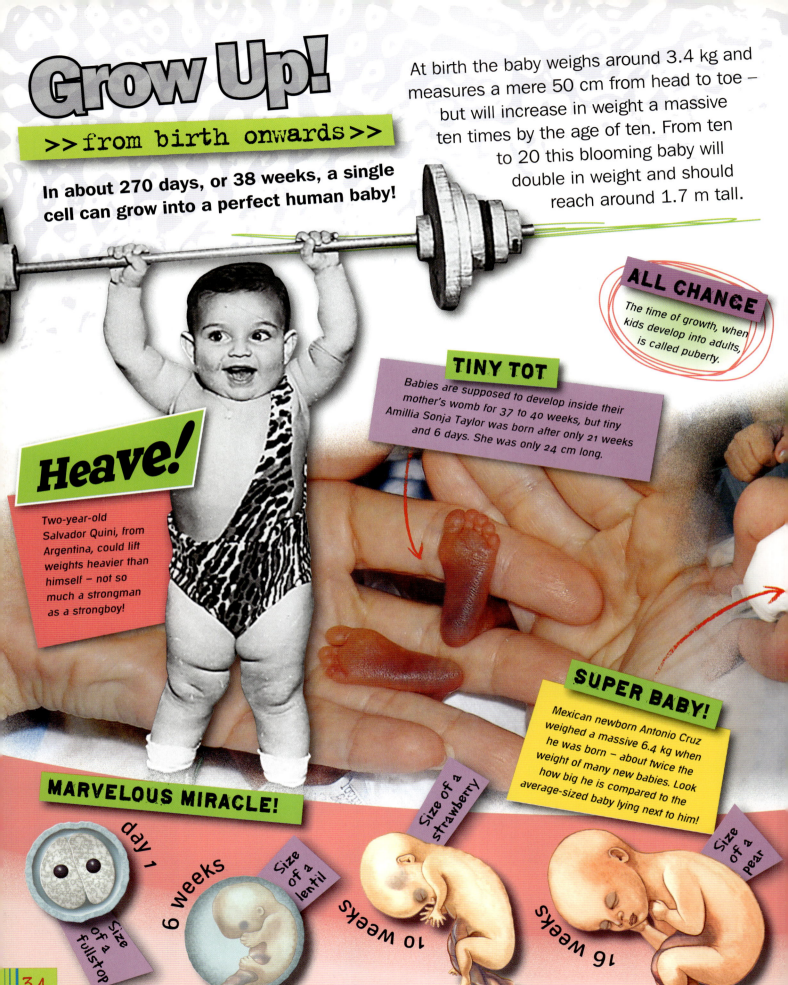

Ageing is a one-way road, which eventually leads to death. Most people can expect to live into their seventies, although there are some supercentenarians (aged over 110 years) alive today.

WORLD'S OLDEST

George Blair – or 'Banana George' to his friends – is the world's oldest barefoot waterskiier. Age hasn't stopped him trying new challenges: he learned to snowboard when he was 75, drove his first racing car aged 81, and made his first parachute jump at 82!

ALL AGES

Three babies are born into the world every second.

Babies born on the island of Bali are not normally named until they are three months old. Before then, they are all called 'mouse'!

Souleymane Mamam of Toga was just 13 years old when he played a World Cup qualifier match against Zambia.

Thanks to the body's amazing ability to heal and grow, doctors are able to stitch new body parts on to people, including arms and faces. Hearts, lungs and kidneys can also be transplanted.

'Red' Rountree was 80 years old when he first decided to rob a bank in the USA. He carried on with his life of crime until he was 92, when he was finally locked up in prison!

twist it!

38 weeks

The baby is developed and ready to be born in the next few days or weeks.

30 weeks

The baby can now hear its mother talking.

22 weeks

The baby can open and close its eyes, and has eyelashes.

Circle of life...

The time from birth to death and the way that humans reproduce (have babies) is called a life cycle.

Do people with big noses smell more? Better ask Mehmet Ozyurek from Turkey – his huge honker measures 8.8 cm. an impressive

No way!

The Long and Short of it

>>all shapes and sizes>>

Breaking news! When it comes to bodies, none of us is 100% 'normal'. The simple fact is every one of us is unique – different and totally special.

From big noses to big toes and bulgy brains to bulgy biceps, your body grows by following a set of rules laid down by your DNA. Found in every cell of your body, DNA is a code for life that's packed with between 20,000 and 30,000 instructions, called genes.

How you turn out isn't just down to DNA though; it's about environment too. That means that the way you choose to live your life will affect your body, mind and health.

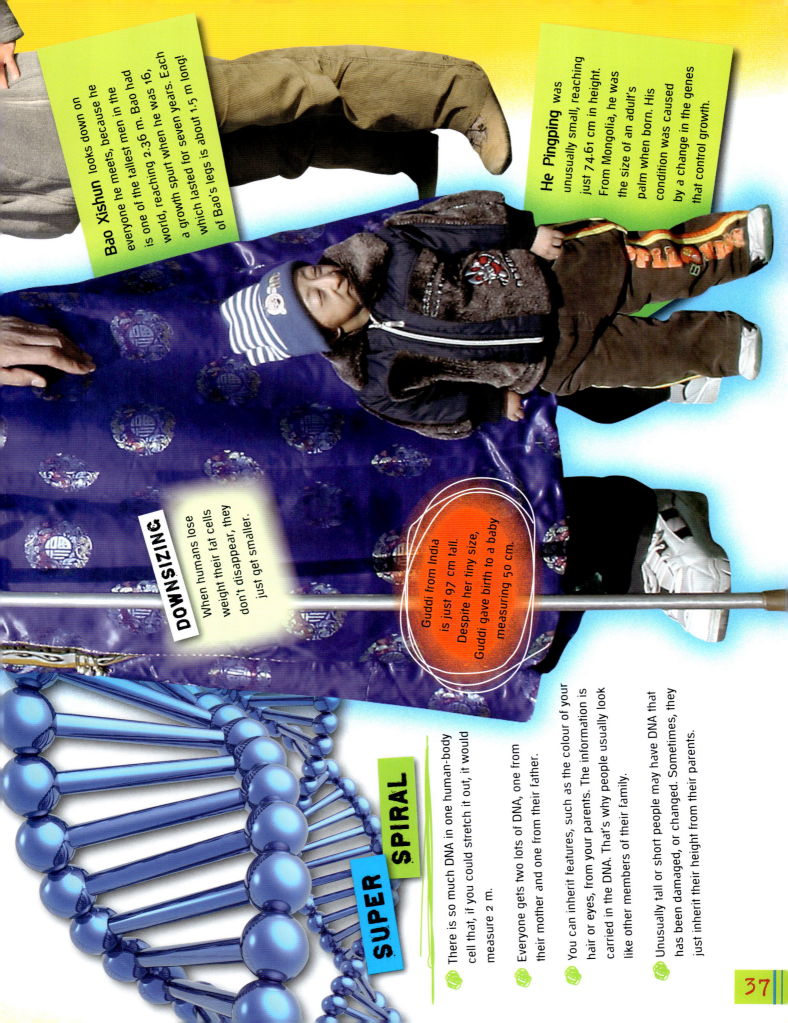

Bao Xishun looks down on everyone he meets, because he is one of the tallest men in the world, reaching 2.36 m. Bao had a growth spurt when he was 16, which lasted for seven years. Each of Bao's legs is about 1.5 m long!

He Pingping was unusually small, reaching just 74.61 cm in height. From Mongolia, he was the size of an adult's palm when born. His condition was caused by a change in the genes that control growth.

DOWNSIZING

When humans lose weight their fat cells don't disappear, they just get smaller.

Guddi from India is just 97 cm tall. Despite her tiny size, Guddi gave birth to a baby measuring 50 cm.

SUPER SPIRAL

- There is so much DNA in one human-body cell that, if you could stretch it out, it would measure 2 m.

- Everyone gets two lots of DNA, one from their mother and one from their father.

- You can inherit features, such as the colour of your hair or eyes, from your parents. The information is carried in the DNA. That's why people usually look like other members of their family.

- Unusually tall or short people may have DNA that has been damaged, or changed. Sometimes, they just inherit their height from their parents.

Mind Reading

Brains are always busy, controlling every body bit including your circulatory system, digestive system, nervous system, senses and feelings.

Your brain is like a lump of warm jelly to touch, but don't be fooled by its cunning disguise. This unbelievable organ contains the very essence of you: your thoughts, dreams, memories, hopes and desires. It's home to your amazing, incredible, magical mind!

Every brain is wrapped in a bony case called a skull, which protects its 100+ billion cells. These cells can handle more than 86 million bits of information a day and your memory can hold at least 100 trillion facts during your lifetime – which is the same as a 1,000 gigabyte computer!

This bit deals with movement.

The front of the brain is in charge of personality, thinking and behaviour.

This is where the brain works on sight and hearing.

The brain is divided into different areas with different jobs to do. For example, there are particular areas that control speech, movement, vision and hearing.

This bit controls sleep and growth.

This area controls balance and coordination.

This is where the brain identifies sounds.

Spinal cord

Stephen Wiltshire has an incredible talent for drawing and can produce remarkably accurate and detailed pictures solely from memory. In 2001, after flying in a helicopter over London, he drew in three hours an aerial illustration of a ten-square-km area of the city, featuring 12 landmarks and 200 other buildings, all in perfect perspective and scale.

These brain cells help to feed and repair the brain. They are shaped like stars.

Everybody can boost their brain's brilliance by reading, learning, playing and exercising. Eating a healthy diet helps too.

Dominic O'Brien has won the World Memory Championships eight times. In 2002 he memorised 54 packs of shuffled cards and remembered each card – all 2,808 of them – in almost perfect order. It took more than four hours to recite them, and he made just eight mistakes!

Ripley's Believe It or Not!®
A bit mental!

A brain weighs about 1.4 kg but if all the water it contains were squeezed out, it would weigh just 283 g!

Unborn babies grow new brain cells at the rate of 250,000 every minute!

For its size, a brain needs up to ten times more energy to work than any other organ.

The brain is one of the few body parts that cannot carry out any movements at all, since it has no muscle tissue.

There is no feeling in the human brain, only in the membrane surrounding it, which contains veins, arteries, and nerves. So a person would feel no pain from an injury to the brain alone.

At the age of 60 a person's brain holds four times more information than it did at the age of 21.

Lights Out

Your eyelids are drooping, your arms and legs feel heavy, and you know it's time to get some shut-eye. Sleep is nature's way of giving all those hard-working body bits of yours some well-earned rest.

The good news is that when the thinking part of your brain hits the snooze button, the other parts that control important jobs – like breathing – stay wide awake!

Most people spend around one third of their lives asleep. Some of that time is spent in a deep sleep, but some of it is also spent dreaming. If you're unlucky, a few of those dreams may turn to nightmares!

LIGHT ON YOUR FEET

Shh! Don't wake your family when you need to get up in the middle of the night – wear these slippers with torches in the toes and you can see where you're going without banging into things!

You've been sitting still, doing very little, when the urge to yawn suddenly takes over. It's your body's way of getting more oxygen into your lungs, so you are ready for action.

NAP ATTACK

The longest anyone has survived without sleep is 18 days, 21 hours and 40 minutes. The woeful wide awaker suffered from memory loss and hallucinations (that means seeing imaginary things).

New parents lose between 400 and 750 hours of sleep in the first year of their baby's life.

Teenagers and young children need about ten hours of sleep a night.

Snails can sleep for long periods of time – up to three years!

Stephen Hearn crashed his car at 113 km/h when he was sleepwalking near Birmingham, England. When he was found, he was in his pyjamas and still snoring.

Sleepwalker Lee Hadwin of North Wales is a good artist when he is asleep, but when awake he struggles to draw at all! Wandering round the house in his sleep he draws everywhere – even on walls and tables!

twist it!

WAY TO GLOW!

A pillow with a built-in light allows its users to read in bed and also acts as an alarm clock. The light can be set to come on gradually at the time you want to wake up. The increasing lightness acts like a sunrise and wakes up sleepyheads in a more natural way than the blare of an alarm or radio.

Your brain needs sleep to be able to work properly. Without sleep you'd find it hard to think clearly, remember anything or keep yourself safe.

BIG WORD ALERT!

SOMNAMBULISTS

It's not unusual for people – especially children – to walk or talk in their sleep. Sleepwalkers are called somnambulists.

ANIMALS SLEEP TOO

Pythons sleep for around 18 hours out of 24, but sheep only need about four hours of sleep.

ICE HOTEL!!

Fancy sleeping on an ice bed? You can do this in Shimukappu, Japan, where an ice hotel caters for sleeping, eating and bathing – all on ice.

Zzzz

SHUT-EYE!

Your eyelids close when you are feeling drowsy. When you dream your eyeballs flick from side to side.

SNORE!

The back of your mouth and throat relax and may partly block your airways, leading to that pig-snuffle snoring sound!

GROW!

While you snooze your body can repair itself and put spare energy into growing.

DREAM!

No one really knows why we dream, but it may help us to organise our thoughts and remember stuff.

RELAX!

Your muscles relax. When you dream, the ability to move your limbs is (usually) switched off – which stops you from acting out your dreams. If this doesn't happen you may find yourself sleepwalking.

Under Attack

You may not know it, but your body is engaged in a deadly battle with the world, right now! It's true – there are plenty of bugs, bacteria and other baddies out there, just waiting to do you harm.

Thankfully, the human body has evolved over millions of years to repel most invaders. Your body has an amazing ability to defend itself, and even repair damage done to it. Without this ability even a simple cold could spell the end of you. Of course, we can't always do it alone, so it's time to say a big 'thank you' to doctors!

Your body fights attackers 24/7. From your tough outer layer – skin – to spit, strong stomach juices, bacteria in your gut, hair in your nose and tears in your eyes, there are lots of clever defence systems in place.

BIG WORD ALERT!

IMMUNE SYSTEM
Your body has an immune system, which makes white blood cells that attack and kill invaders, such as the virus that causes flu.

BUG ALERT!
A VIRUS ATTACKS THE BLOOD STREAM

Vomiting, sneezing, crying, spitting, coughing and diarrhoea (runny faeces) are all ways of chucking out stuff your body doesn't like.

TASTY!

These tiny fish nibble at dead skin on customers' feet at a spa resort in Japan – and leave the feet clean and refreshed!

TOASTY!

Stand back! This fire treatment is popular in China to help prevent colds and flu.

MUDDY!

It's a mucky business in these mud baths, which are meant to ease pain and diseases.

KILL OR CURE

In ancient times, headaches and other medical problems were sometimes cured by drilling holes into the skull. Known as 'trepanation' this operation is still carried out in some parts of the world today.

Maggots are sometimes used to treat infected skin and tissues, which they eat. Because they don't eat healthy flesh, these greedy grubs help wounds to heal before life-threatening infections, such as gangrene, can set in.

A pair of spiders set up home inside the ear canal of nine-year-old Jesse Courtney from America. Thankfully, doctors were able to extract the eight-legged invaders, and no harm was done.

Over 2,000 years ago, Hippocrates, a doctor, told his patients to chew on bark from a willow tree when they were in pain. We now use an ingredient found in willow bark to make aspirin!

twist it!

OLD BONES

In some Chinese villages, dinosaur bones are ground up to make a paste. It's used to treat dizziness and leg cramps!

in the olden days

Before modern medical science took over, people invented some weird ways to get better.

CATCH THAT SHREW!

Aching bones were treated with the help of a dead shrew. Sufferers were told to keep the furry little creatures in their pockets.

DON'T BE AN ASS!

Passing a child under the belly of a donkey three times was said to cure whooping cough.

HOT AND STEAMING!

If you had TB – a deadly chest disease – you'd be told to kill a cow, stick your head into its warm body, and breathe in deeply.

TOM FOR YOUR TUM!

One of the first types of tomato ketchup was used to cure diarrhoea in the 1800s.

Muntoyib, an Indonesian bee-sting therapist, covers himself with hundreds of live honeybees in India. Some people think that bee venom injected from live stinging bees helps treat chronic pain.

Fit for Life

>>take care>>

There's no such thing as a perfect human, but keeping your body bits in tip-top shape has got to make good sense.

The human body is like a mighty machine with lots of working parts. It needs to be taken care of – and that means exercise and a good diet. There are around six billion humans on the planet, and many of them, from super-sized sumo wrestlers to bendy-bodied yogis, keep the power switch turned to maximum.

For kids, it's easy to keep it fun. All you've got to do is play, eat well and sleep. But for some groaning grown-ups, it's a hard, sweaty slog keeping those muscles and bones in peak condition.

GULP!

Water makes up 60% of your body weight. It's the liquid of life, so drink up. Your bones and teeth are packed with calcium – there's loads of this mighty mineral in milk.

GRUB!

Veggies and fruit are great grub. At least one-third of a human's diet should be made up of these super foods.

GO FOR IT!

Squash – the hard-hitting racquet and ball game – has been voted the healthiest sport ever, beating running, swimming and basketball into first place.

FITNESS FUN

Hula hooping is a hu-lotta fun! Alesya Goulevich spun 100 hula hoops at the same time, at the Big Apple Circus in Boston in 2004.

SURF'S UP!

Surfers are super-fit because they use almost every muscle in their bodies to stay balanced and upright on their boards.

PUSHING IT

Ashrita Furman, a health-food store manager from New York City, is super fit. Amongst his amazing feats are climbing Mount Fuji on a pogo stick, hula hooping with a 4.46-m hoop, and doing 9,628 sit ups in an hour. Here, he's pushing an orange along for one mile using his nose!

twist it!

You're never too young to get fit! In 2006 1,100 babies took part in a crawling marathon. The mini racers had to crawl along a 5-m track, and the young winner was rewarded with a bag of baby goodies!

Aged 91, Ervin Ashley of the USA climbed 2,000 steps every day to keep in shape!

Cycling backwards is a popular sport in some parts of the world. Riders sit on the handlebars and pedal in reverse.

Tirtha Kumar Phani from India ran more than 60 km every day, for one year. He clocked up a blistering 22,581 km in total!

FITNESS FANATICS

Kids should be exercising for at least 60 minutes every day. Running, walking, cycling and playing sports all keep you fit for life.

stick with it!

Kyle Nolte from Arkansas has got so good at jumping on his pogo stick, he can also play baseball, hula hoop or skip whilst pogoing!

HUMAN BODY INDEX

46

ACKNOWLEDGEMENTS

COVER (l) © Sebastian Kaulitzki – istockphoto.com, (r) Lilli Strauss/AP/PA Photos; **2** (r) Raymond w. Gonzales, (t/l) © Peter Galbraith – fotolia.com; **4** © Sebastian Kaulitzki – istockphoto.com; **5** (t/r) Lilli Strauss/AP/PA Photos; **6–7** (dp) © AlienCat – fotolia.com; **7** (b/l) Raymond W Gonzales, (b/r) Simon De Trey-White/ Barcroft Media; **8** (r) © Peter Galbraith – fotolia.com, (l) © AlienCat – fotolia.com; **9** (l, b) ChinaFotoPress/Photocome/PA Photos; **10** (sp) © V. Yakobchuk – fotolia.com; **11** (c) © Sebastian Kaulitzki – istockphoto.com, (r) © Wong Sze Fei – fotolia.com; **13** (l) © Roman Dekan – fotolia.com, (t/r) AP Photo/Rubin Museum of Art, Diane Bondareff, (b/r) Jeff Chen/Trigger images; **15** (b/r) © saginbay – fotolia.com; **14–15** (b) © Xtremer – fotolia.com, (c) © saginbay – fotolia.com; **17** (l) Patrick Hertzog/AFP/Getty Images, (c) Prakash Hatvalne/AP/PA Photos, (r) Reuters/Christina Hu; **18** (t/l) Reuters/ Seth Wenig, (b/l) Camera Press/Terje Eggum/Scanpix; **18–19** (b/c) © ktsdesign – fotolia.com; **21** (l) Manichi Rafi, (b) Steven Heward/toothartist.com, (t/r) Fabian Bimmer/AP/PA Photos; **22** (l) Dr. Kessel & Dr. Kardon/Tissues & Organs/ Getty Images, (b) Reuters/Staff Photographer; **23** (t/r) Nils Jorgensen/Rex Features, (b) Matt Cardy/Getty Images, (b/r) Stan Honda/AFP/Getty Images; **24–25** (c) © Mark Kostich – istockphoto.com; **25** (c/r) Sipa Press/Rex Features, (b/r) Phil Noble/PA Archive/PA Photos, (t/r) Reuters/STR New; **27** (l) Dan Burton/underwaterimages.co.uk, (t/r) John Bavosi/Science Photo Library, (b/r) Gabriel Bouys/AFP/Getty Images; **28** (l) © Sebastian Kaulitzki – fotolia.com; **29** (l) Roger Bamber/Rex Features, (r) Tim Barnsley/Armidale Express; **30** (r) NBCUPhotobank/Rex Features; **31** (t) Ian Waldie/Rex Features, (r) Scott Barbour/Getty Images; **32** (l) Jean/Empics Entertainment, (r) Thanh Nien Newspaper/AP/PA Photos; **33** (l) Rex Features, (r) Tao-Chuan Yeh/AFP/Getty Images; **34** (r) Reuters/Ho New; **35** (l) Reuters/Victor Ruiz, (r) George A. Blair; **36–37** (dp) Reuters/China Daily China Daily Information Corp; **36** (t/l) IHA/UPPA/Photoshot; **37** (l) © Dmitry Sunagatov – fotolia.com, (t) © Sasha Radosavljevic – istockphoto.com; **39** (t) Gary Bishop/Rex Features, (b) Greg Williams/Rex Features, (r) © Sebastian Kaulitzki – fotolia.com; **40–41** (dp) © Veronika Vasilyuk – fotolia.com; **40** (c) Rex Features; **41** (t/r) Solent News/Rex Features, (b) Reuters/ Kim Kyung Hoon; **42** (sp) © David Marchal – istockphoto.com; **43** (t/l) Reuters/Larry Downing, (t/c) Chu Yongzhi/ ChinaFotoPress/GettyImages, (t/r) Reuters/China Daily China Daily Information Corp – CDIC, (b) Reuters/Beawiharta Beawiharta; **44–45** (b) Reuters/Sergio Moraes; **44** (t) Boston Herald/Rex Features; **45** (l) Reuters/Shannon Stapleton

Key: t = top, b = bottom, c = centre, l = left, r = right, sp = single page, dp = double page, bgd = background

All other photos are from Ripley Entertainment Inc.

All artwork by Janet Baker & Julian Baker (JB Illustrations)

Every attempt has been made to acknowledge correctly and contact copyright holders and we apologise in advance for any unintentional errors or omissions, which will be corrected in future editions.